To Little Thing One and Little Thing Two,
Emile and Mason

First published in the United States of America in 2001
by UNIVERSE PUBLISHING
A Division of Rizzoli International Publications, Inc.
300 Park Avenue South, New York, New York 10010

© 2001 Thames & Hudson Ltd, London
Text © 2001 Phyllis Richardson

ISBN 0-7893-0642-5

2002 2003 2004 2005 / 10 9 8 7 6 5 4 3 2

Printed in Singapore

Library of Congress Control Number 2001089894

Phyllis Richardson
Edited by Lucas Dietrich

XS:
Big Ideas,
Small Buildings

Universe

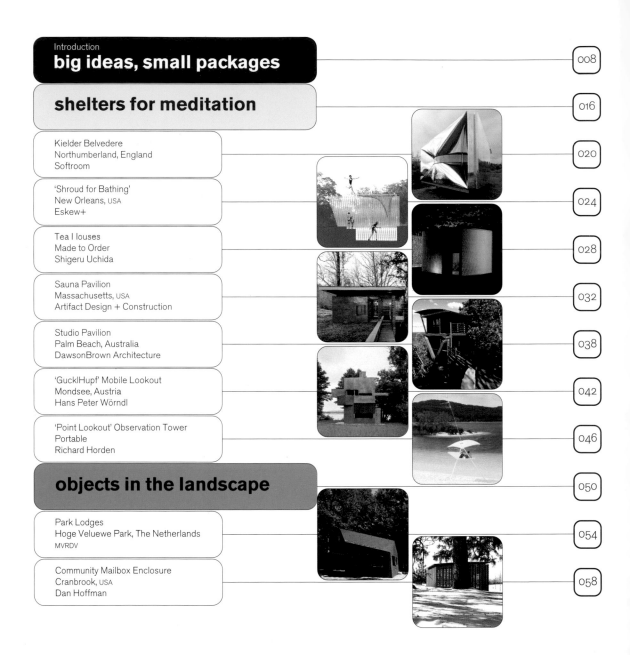

Introduction
big ideas, small packages
008

shelters for meditation
016

Kielder Belvedere
Northumberland, England
Softroom
020

'Shroud for Bathing'
New Orleans, USA
Eskew+
024

Tea Houses
Made to Order
Shigeru Uchida
028

Sauna Pavilion
Massachusetts, USA
Artifact Design + Construction
032

Studio Pavilion
Palm Beach, Australia
DawsonBrown Architecture
038

'GucklHupf' Mobile Lookout
Mondsee, Austria
Hans Peter Wörndl
042

'Point Lookout' Observation Tower
Portable
Richard Horden
046

objects in the landscape
050

Park Lodges
Hoge Veluewe Park, The Netherlands
MVRDV
054

Community Mailbox Enclosure
Cranbrook, USA
Dan Hoffman
058

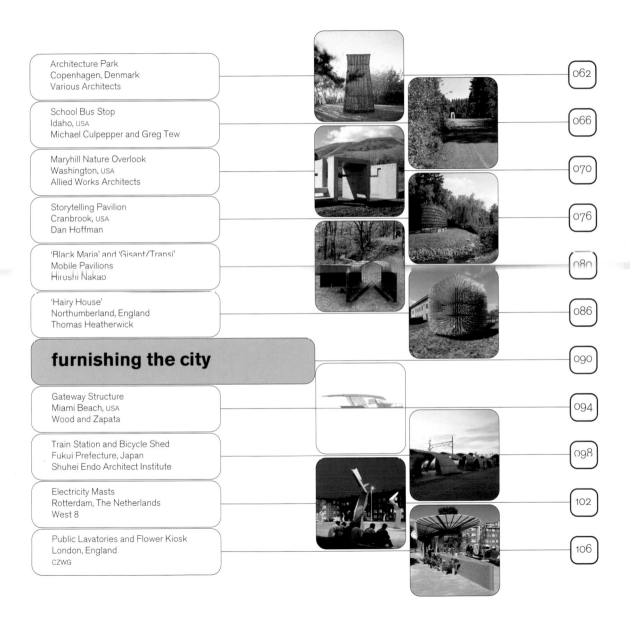

Architecture Park
Copenhagen, Denmark
Various Architects — 062

School Bus Stop
Idaho, USA
Michael Culpepper and Greg Tew — 066

Maryhill Nature Overlook
Washington, USA
Allied Works Architects — 070

Storytelling Pavilion
Cranbrook, USA
Dan Hoffman — 076

'Black Maria' and 'Gisant/Transi'
Mobile Pavilions
Hiroshi Nakao — 080

'Hairy House'
Northumberland, England
Thomas Heatherwick — 086

furnishing the city

090

Gateway Structure
Miami Beach, USA
Wood and Zapata — 094

Train Station and Bicycle Shed
Fukui Prefecture, Japan
Shuhei Endo Architect Institute — 098

Electricity Masts
Rotterdam, The Netherlands
West 8 — 102

Public Lavatories and Flower Kiosk
London, England
CZWG — 106

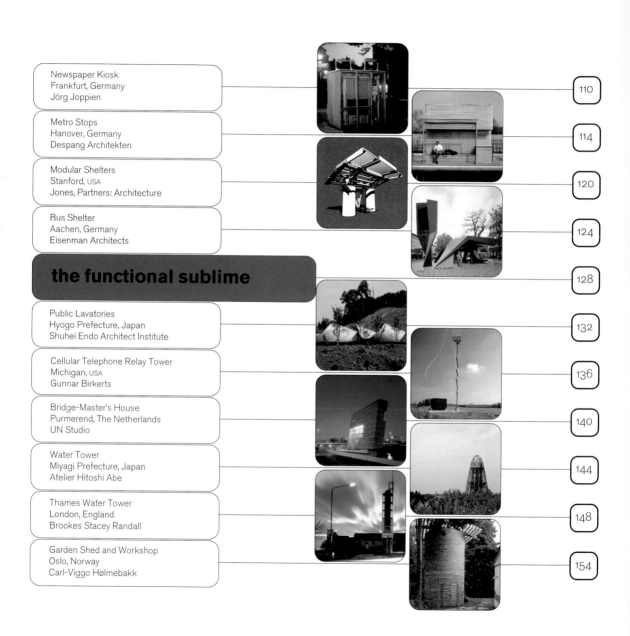

Newspaper Kiosk
Frankfurt, Germany
Jörg Joppien

110

Metro Stops
Hanover, Germany
Despang Architekten

114

Modular Shelters
Stanford, USA
Jones, Partners: Architecture

120

Bus Shelter
Aachen, Germany
Eisenman Architects

124

the functional sublime

128

Public Lavatories
Hyogo Prefecture, Japan
Shuhei Endo Architect Institute

132

Cellular Telephone Relay Tower
Michigan, USA
Gunnar Birkerts

136

Bridge-Master's House
Purmerend, The Netherlands
UN Studio

140

Water Tower
Miyagi Prefecture, Japan
Atelier Hitoshi Abe

144

Thames Water Tower
London, England
Brookes Stacey Randall

148

Garden Shed and Workshop
Oslo, Norway
Carl-Viggo Hølmebakk

154

anytime, anywhere

158

'Icos' Treetop Observation Structure
Portable
Gilles Ebersolt

162

'Su-Si and Fred'
Made to Order
Kaufmann 96 Architektur

166

'Ski Haus' Alpine Station
Portable
Richard Horden

172

'La Ballule' Inflatable Sphere
Portable
Gilles Ebersolt

178

Mountain Cabins
California, USA
Jones, Partners: Architecture

182

'Silva Spider' and 'Fisch Haus'
Portable
Richard Horden

186

'Rotation Pneu' Shelter
Portable
Dominik Baumüller

192

Floating Pavilion
Groningen, The Netherlands
Maki and Associates

196

'Maison-Valise' Housing Unit
Portable
TimeZone

200

'Basic House'
Portable
Martin Ruiz de Azúa

204

sources
Project Credits • Architect Information
Index • Picture Credits

208

big ideas, small packages

'Too small to live in and too large to hang on a
watch chain'
     Anonymous (said of Chiswick House, London)

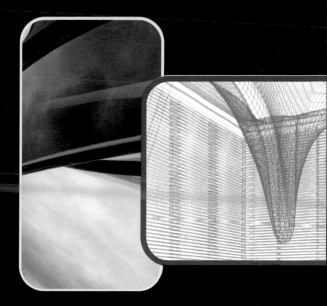

Small buildings have always had a particular appeal. From
the diminutive temples created by the ancient Greeks to
the follies of the English romantic landscape, micro works
of architecture inspire an enduring fascination that
transgresses their function, even if that function is to be a
pleasing decoration in a landscape. There are a variety of
reasons for our love-affair with little forms. Most obviously,
the miniaturization of architecture reduces it to a human
scale with which we can interact more readily. We are
also drawn by the intricacy of their conception and detail
and by the fact that smaller buildings usually possess a
more tactile quality than constructions of larger scale. The
concise purpose of these structures, that they address
a single function, simple use or even a purely aesthetic
aim, makes them psychologically as well as physically
accessible. And yet that is not to say that they are
static expressions.

     For centuries architects have used the small form to
experiment with space on a reduced scale, to explore the
details of construction, the joy of materials and play of
form. Although the design of even a modest house
contains programmatic complexities, architects trying to
achieve simplicity and unity of form and function find
themselves faced with the ultimate design question, and it

is perhaps in the built answers that we can experience
the architect's vision at its most distilled. A superb
example of early experimentation in a small building that
reflected one of the finest manifestations of the High
Renaissance was the early-seventeenth-century
tempietto of San Pietro in Montorio, Rome, built by
Bramante. However miniature in size, the tempietto
reflects a lofty goal: the reconciliation of humanist, pagan
and Christian ideals in a single built feat. Although the
building had no concrete function, its circular plan
conjures a celebration of the universal spirit – 'an image
of the world', as Andrea Palladio would have had it. But

the building is much more than a temple of good will: its deceptively simple geometry belies a complex mathematical formulation developed by Bramante that imbues the whole with a vitality and mystery that has an immediate and lasting appeal to anyone who comes in contact with it. In their different ways, all the buildings here aspire to the same end.

But despite the care and thought that little buildings embody, they are often overlooked or taken for granted in today's ever more urbanized, global culture. In a rural setting, small structures are associated with the ornamental garden folly, a whimsical presence to be 'discovered' in the lush natural landscape. In an urban context, small buildings and functional structures are dwarfed by monumental civic architecture and the focus on function can take precedence over beauty. It may be easier to appreciate little buildings in the tranquillity of the landscape, where function is perhaps less important and contemplation is more readily induced, but either way, the small structure struggles to establish its significance against a backdrop of increasingly grand architectural gestures. The architects whose work is shown here have chosen to explore serious themes within a small but infinitely elastic framework in which detail, function, form, dynamism, material and proportion can be brought to a logical and pleasing conclusion.

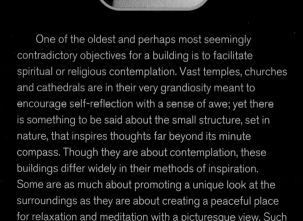

One of the oldest and perhaps most seemingly contradictory objectives for a building is to facilitate spiritual or religious contemplation. Vast temples, churches and cathedrals are in their very grandiosity meant to encourage self-reflection with a sense of awe; yet there is something to be said about the small structure, set in nature, that inspires thoughts far beyond its minute compass. Though they are about contemplation, these buildings differ widely in their methods of inspiration. Some are as much about promoting a unique look at the surroundings as they are about creating a peaceful place for relaxation and meditation with a picturesque view. Such

buildings signify that our urge in the modern age to invade and conquer the land has been somewhat supplanted by a strong desire to consider ourselves critically in the environment. Unlike larger constructions, these shelters, overlooks and eyries present a humble face to their natural setting, frequently in celebration of that setting so that it rather than the structure becomes the focus of the architectural exercise. These buildings are self-conscious of their own intrusion upon the topography, though in their design and execution they contribute to, rather than detract from, the glory of the landscapes they inhabit.

Similarly, when we see the standard of these modern-day follies, we have to agree that they are an improvement on the adornments placed on the eighteenth-century estates under the grand shadows of the English country house. Some of these structures here are in fact not without function, nor do they strive to mimic larger works in miniaturized doll-house versions. The folly aspect has more to do with the playful quality and inventiveness that structures of a reduced scale naturally exude. All of the follies and pavilions shown here intentionally straddle the boundary between art and architecture. Some are unquestionably sculptural objects that beckon the observer to enter and explore the tactile materials and light effects within and about the built

piece. Others possess an inherent beauty that enhances, but does not determine or impede, their function. They attain the wonderful status of art forms that could and should exist for their aesthetic quality alone, though many offer the added benefit of utility.

Blurring boundaries is an important theme that runs through all of these projects, which is why some could be featured in more than one chapter. There are numerous precedents in the fusion of functionality and portability, of formal beauty and folly, of urban industry and do-it-yourself, but it is perhaps Buckminster Fuller's research into cost-effective, efficient, structurally elegant solutions for a broad range of design-related problems that has captured the imagination of the widest range of architects. In particular, his Dymaxion Deployment Unit (1940), commissioned by the British War Relief Organization, drew on design principles that he had applied at both the micro (automobiles) and macro (high-rises) scale. Originally conceived as small, single-family dwellings, the design was modified by Fuller during war time for emergency use. Employing the same kind of self-supporting bent sheet metal seen in middle American grain silos, as well as their circular plan, the units were inexpensive to manufacture and eminently transportable. By melding mass-produced materials and structural ingenuity, Fuller's contributions have become an invaluable source of inspiration. Many of these buildings demonstrate the use of lightweight industrial materials and the pursuit of the self-contained, independent structure, evidence of the influence and rewards of such experimentation in design on a reduced scale.

Attempts to reconcile form and function have also produced a fair amount of experimental architecture, some more successful than others. Pure function is at its most manifest in urban contexts. Although city dwellers rarely appreciate or enjoy the street furniture that surrounds them, many pieces of street furniture and infrastructure are the result of a great deal of consideration and research. Examples of truly usable and ultimately user-friendly architecture that bring a nod of appreciation from the man in the street have become rarefied the world over, whether because of bureaucratic apathy or artistic timidity.

In the late 1950s and 1960s, the creative movement known as the Situationist International projected an ideal city in which small-scale urban interventions would produce chance encounters between people and objects. Today we should realize that even the most uninspired small projects, such as bus shelters, public lavatories, kiosks, market stalls, can be animated by the imagination of a good architect. Some designs might seem like attempts to reinvent the wheel, but if so, they have succeeded in producing something much smaller, more efficient and a joy to behold. Clever design and attention to detail, especially when applied to the elements of our urban or suburban landscape, produce works that become much-needed positive micro-expressions of the aims and aspirations of the community at large.

At the highest level, as many of these structures demonstrate, these objects can be interesting,

provocative and even go so far as to blend art and architecture in a cohesive and aesthetically pleasing whole. To achieve this, many architects have had to overcome or even ignored constraints of size, definition, budget and municipal monotony to produce works that are robustly utilitarian and beautifully innovative, placeless and timeless.

Though in the twenty-first century our aspirations and indeed our addresses may be increasingly in a state of flux, we can still strive for beauty. It is therefore fitting to consider an array of mobile structures that confront the issue of transience, suggesting that it is an ecologically sound and ideal human condition – and one that can be enhanced by good design. Structures that come ready to assemble, that can be erected and disassembled in a matter of hours, and those that have the least impact on

the natural environment while providing adequate shelter and modern amenities, are the preoccupation of several architects whose ambitions are not only toward the micro but the autonomous. Here the emphasis is on a multiplicity of functions. As several architects have produced structures that rely on the principles of tensegrity for support, it seems appropriate to look again to Buckminster Fuller, who said that the home must 'as completely as possible be independent and self supporting, have its own character, dignity, and beauty or harmony'. So while it appears that the *grands projets* of the past still have a place in our current culture, there is a trend toward accommodating future generations, not by outdoing

This book is a celebration of the little things in life, those unexpected objects that make us momentarily pause to ponder their meaning, or our own meaning, or simply to appreciate the elegance of their creation. From the spectrum of functions and styles of these buildings, it is utterly clear that size imposes no limits on creativity and utility is no constraint to beauty. Thinking small can be a wonderfully constructive exercise.

'XS' is a play on letters intended to conjure the aura of whimsy that surrounds these generally purposeful buildings. All are exceptional examples of how every object, no matter how tiny or how functional, and no matter where they are, can bring a little joy. And that is no small achievement.

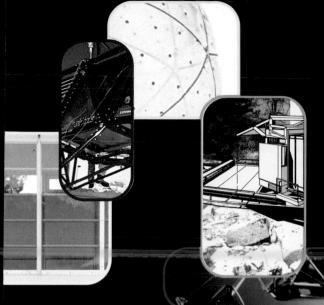

what has been done before but by doing less, though in the most progressive, ecologically sensitive and craft-conscious way.

In 2000 the American magazine *Architecture* devoted an issue to 'the Primitive Hut'; later that year France's *l'Architecture d'Aujourd'hui* dedicated a volume to 'Micro-Architecture' with meditations on the cabin, the small room, the fairytale cottage. Could it be that as our world becomes increasingly global, we find satisfaction, or at least sanity, in concentrating our attentions and desires on a small, personalized habitation or shelter? Perhaps as the world expands through our television and computer screens, our instinct is to look for somewhere intimate for refuge, not in defiance but in self-reflection and complete apprehension.

shelters
for
meditation

Lookouts, eyries and inspiring nature huts

Whether intended to block out urban clatter or to commune with the natural environment, structures that mediate nature and the appreciation of that natural world through their walls and roofs take a variety of forms: bunkers that bury themselves in the earth, perfectly positioned panoramic lookouts that take in an untouched rural setting, primitive huts that return us to our essential beings. The aim of this splendid isolation is manifold: to observe, to contemplate, to become inspired or calmed.

Architects who demonstrate a reverence for the landscape, and sensitivity to their impact on their surroundings are heartening in a time of serious ecological concerns. The challenges for designers and architects with such an awareness are several: how to create environmentally and visually friendly buildings and how to respond to the sweeping drama of a landscape or an untrammelled wilderness in a manner that enhances nature and our experience of it.

In view of this complex relationship, it is not surprising that small shelters in the landscape have a somewhat mythical history. From tales of fairy cottages to Marc-Antoine Laugier's observations on the primitive hut as Ur-architecture, a rich narrative of buildings in nature exists. Perhaps it is because man feels dwarfed by the grandeur of the natural world that we find the 'humanized' scale exemplified by the projects presented here so appealing. Concerned with leaving the smallest footprint, these designs aspire toward the compact to heighten the perception of the surroundings, particularly the presence of water, which always provides a sense of limitlessness and grandiosity. Some structures, like Softroom's 'belvedere', which overlooks the barren expanse of Kielder Water in the north of England, and Richard Horden's 'Point Lookout', designed for observation of beaches, were created specifically for water-related use. The mirror-sided belvedere serves as a resting place and beacon for walkers awaiting ferries, while Horden's gracefully angled observation tower is intended for use by rescue crews and nature lovers.

Employing the view of the water to orient and complement their structures, Austrian architect Hans Peter Wörndl set his multiplaned 'GucklHupf' on the bank of the Mondsee River, and Robert Brown created a studio on stilts to take in vistas of Australia's Palm Beach and the Pacific Ocean. Wörndl's wood box is actually a mobile unit that can be disassembled and reconstructed with relative ease, and once fully erected, the little structure can be configured through an array of opening and closing planes. The idea was to create not a static object but one capable of transforming itself within an ever-mutating setting. Similarly, to acknowledge man's intrusion upon wild settings,

'Point Lookout' was designed to be carried into a place where permanent constructions are not allowed, erected, then taken down after use, as if it had never touched the earth.

Internalizing the experience of water, a bathing pavilion designed by Eskew+ contains a pool and space for quiet meditation that celebrates the elements of earth, air and water through open-plank walls and a specially woven roof fabric that captures rain-water, which in turn is 'dripped' slowly into the pool. This 'shroud for bathing' literally embodies permeability, transparency and groundedness. Likewise, Artifact Design's sauna pavilion, set on a quiet lakeside in rural Massachusetts, reaches out into water, uniting built and unbuilt in a sympathetic interplay of forms and materials.

Though you might want to place one near a favourite body of water, Shigeru Uchida's do-it-yourself tea houses are not site specific, but they share with the other structures a concentration on an idea, philosophy or practice beyond the building or its inhabitants. In this case, it is the time-honoured ritual of the Japanese tea ceremony that focuses the mind and encourages thoughts beyond the physical shelter. Uchida concerns himself with 'inner design', not the object itself but the space created within the object, a lesson that minimizing the size and volume of a structure can have a converse effect on perception.

shining star

Kielder Belvedere
Northumberland, England
Softroom

An unexpected sparkle in the landscape of Northumberland, the shelter overlooks Kielder Water, the largest man-made lake in northern Europe, turning its back to the vast Northumberland forest. The belvedere offers refuge for walkers in inclement weather and serves as a waiting point for ferry passengers during the summer months. The young London-based practice Softroom won a competition sponsored by the Kielder Partnership, which had established a visual arts programme to create such shelters in the area. The structure took only ten months to produce and was nominated for British Building of the Year 2000 – glittering testimony to the worthwhile cause of public funding for the arts.

Approaching the jewel-like triangular volume from the park, one first encounters the planes of the two etched-steel mirror walls that reflect the forest canopy and are joined by a curved door at the apex. Inside sits a 'golden circular chamber' (stainless-steel walls were powder-coated gold), which is top-lit through a coloured skylight so that a warm, inviting glow counterbalances the exterior's reflective polish. The third side of the triangle, which faces the lakeside, resembles a bulbous square that has been pulled in at the middle to produce a convex surface of two triangles positioned one atop the other.

Across the centre of the lakeside façade runs a band that follows the line of the inner drum and appears to belt the convex shape into the two billowing triangles. When seated on the bench inside the structure, one can enjoy a panoramic view of the lake through a glazed slot within the belt so that, while warm and protected

within the belvedere's solid geometry, walkers can still feel connected to the natural landscape.

The structure's reflective surfaces were intended not to stand out of their own accord but to mirror the 'giant composition of sky, forest and water', though it becomes a strange attractor in that composition when viewed from nearby vantage points. The shiny-smooth surface also conceals the shelter's robustness, which is meant to withstand harsh weather and vandalism. Ultimately, the belvedere's tribute to its surroundings is not to make itself invisible within them but to emphasize their grandeur. Long may it shine.

plan

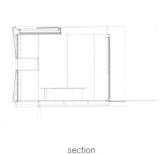

section

[opposite] Entrance is at the apex of two steel mirror walls. The polished stainless steel was used to reflect the forest landscape.
[left] The drawings reveal the circular chamber within the triangular volume.
[below and previous pages] The lakeside elevation features a curved band of glazing that appears to belt the structure and allows views over the vast, man-made lake.

rain drip

'Shroud for Bathing'
New Orleans, USA
Eskew+

Water, light, gauzy fabric, natural wood – Eskew+ has assembled the ingredients for the modern grotto, replacing dark, damp and kitschy with dappled and mellow. Commissioned to produce a private pool and meditation room, the designers seized on the association of the area with rainfall and humidity to create the 'shroud for bathing'. The water drop became a guiding principle for invention of form.

The roof leaks, but only after the fabric, specially woven elastic latex membrane that contains titanium 'for reflective qualities and strength', becomes saturated. Then the special weave of the fabric allows it to expand so that a vertical sack gradually distends as it fills, letting water drip gently into the pool below. A comfortable size (6 x 3.6 metres, 1.2 metres deep) for wading and meditation, the pool is not large enough to suggest a rigorous set of laps. Surrounding the water is a structure composed of stacked cypress slats that filter light while, from within, the bather can glimpse the garden into which the pavilion has been so artfully inserted. A stair has been 'woven' into one side of the wood box to give access to the roof membrane. In an act of visual sleight of hand, the apparently delicate fabric that allows water to seep in is in fact structural: when the weather outside is good, the surface is flat, intended for walking on or for sunbathing.

Setting the shallow, poured-concrete pool within the unusual wood and fabric enclosure achieves both privacy and escape from the New Orleans heat. Although the hanging, dripping fabric imparts a cavelike feeling, the transparent quality of the materials ensures that the sense of being outdoors is not compromised. With the pool dug into the earth, light and air passing between the wood planks and rain-water permeating the roof structure, the bather is never far removed from the elements, in body or mind.

[above and previous page] Timber-slatted sides allow light to penetrate the pavilion, while the woven latex fabric roof is both strong enough to walk on and uniquely permeable. As rain continues to fall, the vertical sack fills with water and drips into the pool below.

[left] The poured-concrete pool is dug into the earth, reinforcing the pavilion's grotto-like character.

tea for three

Tea Houses
Made to Order
Shigeru Uchida

In the sixteenth century the Japanese tea ceremony began to exert an influence on the architecture of the house; an intimate room dedicated to the appreciation of tea and the harmony of the utensils became a must for dwellings of wealthy merchants and nobility to entertain and impress honoured guests. Five hundred years on, Shigeru Uchida has 'translated' the aesthetic of the modern Japanese tea room for a modern European audience. Because he feels that the discipline, principles and philosophy of the Japanese tea ceremony have no parallel in Western culture, he has designed three stand-alone, cube-shaped structures in textured surfaces of bamboo and wood to illuminate, quite literally as they are lit from within, the importance of the ceremony and the space in which it is performed.

The tea houses, though appealing in purity of form and beauty of detail – their delicate constructions bring to mind the craft of paper lanterns – are subservient to the ceremony itself. It is Uchida's aim to draw attention not to his objects but to the space created by the object. The purpose of the ceremony is to focus the mind, and as Uchida argues, 'the shape of the room must not divert from it.' Each design, labelled Ji-An, So-An and Gyo-An (for 'sense and perception', 'concept and composition' and 'will and memory'), has its own range of essential elements, such as brazier, kettle, tea bowl and scoop, lamp, vase and cushion, and each has a specific placement in the house, which includes, according to tradition, separate entrances for host and guest. Though the modular form and easy assembly appear modern and European, the concentration on space more than structure, the domination of physical form by metaphysical contemplation locates Uchida's scheme, if not in Japanese history, then in a more discreet consciousness than contemporary building trends usually suggest.

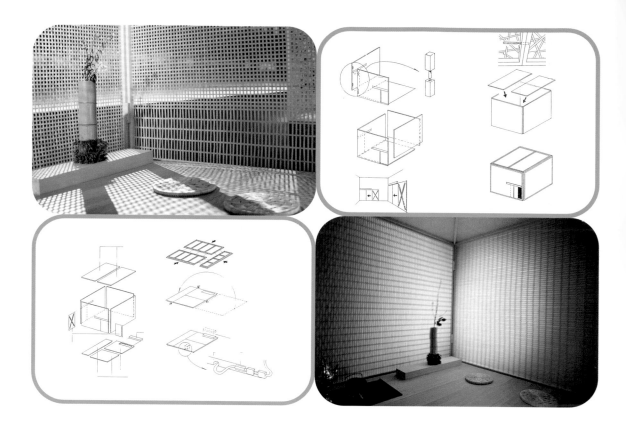

Uchida claims to design not 'isolated objects but the space itself in which the tea ceremony will be performed'. His focus is on 'reduction', in this case reducing the cultural and metaphysical encryptions in the tea ceremony to a simple, potent form.

[left] The three tea houses are individually designed down to the utensils needed for the tea ceremony itself.
[below] The three designs are labelled Ji-An, So-An and Gyo-An ('sense and perception', 'concept and composition' and 'will and memory').

hot house

Sauna Pavilion
Massachusetts, USA
Artifact Design + Construction

It has the immediate look and feel of a small mountain cabin of the kind that has been built in the region for centuries, but that is to its credit as a modern building with distinctly grander architectural aspirations. The small sauna pavilion designed by Sal Tranchina and Chris Kilbridge of Artifact Design + Construction sits quietly in a picturesque lakeside setting that is skirted by the Appalachian Trail in the Berkshire Mountains of Massachusetts. Its restrained low profile and cedar planks offset its modern credentials, while an inventive use of materials – copper cladding in the steam room, split-face concrete block for the retaining wall and quadruple-glazed windows to insulate heat – suggests that there is something beyond the vernacular lurking behind the trees.

On closer inspection the components reveal a building that is as inspired architecturally as it is by the beauty of the natural environment. The rectilinear form and glass planes recall the International Style, and the darkly polished interior, the deck and the 'gangplank' cantilevering toward the lake have more than a hint of the master of Fallingwater.

Yet this structure is its own justification. The design features a 2.4 × 2.4-metre sauna chamber, dressing area, outdoor shower, storage and a walkway-cum-diving

board that invites heated (and intrepid) bodies to refresh themselves in the cooling lake. The genius of the design lies in the way the architects have devoted specific materials to each activity that come together in a coherent and unintrusive whole: the sauna is lined in red cedar but clad in copper, interior floors are green slate, and the outdoor shower is screened by a cedar plank wall. The gangplank is also made of cedar, which along with the copper will blend over time into the surroundings as it weathers. A single square window punched through the sauna room's wall looks out over the lake, the glass and water reflecting back on each other in an act of mutual appreciation.

site plan

[above] The schematic drawing shows the sauna building set well within the surrounding vegetation, with the cedar 'gangplank' extending to the edge of the lake. [top] The exploded form. [right and previous] The earthy tones of the materials – cedar, copper, green slate – and their natural tendency to weather allow the structure to blend harmoniously with the lush surroundings while providing for the necessities of privacy, insulation and hardiness.

a room at the top

Studio Pavilion
Palm Beach, Australia
DawsonBrown Architecture

Restoration work doesn't usually allow much room for invention but Robert Brown didn't need much room for this remarkable timber studio. In the refurbishment and repair of a 1920s cottage on a beach north of Sydney, the architect created an eyrie on stilts that sits like a treehouse among dense foliage and natural rock shelves. The 'delicate yet sturdy' pavilion is accessed by a bridge that spans the cottage pool, enhancing the sense of seclusion but anchoring the small structure to the rest of the scheme. Although conservation was the focus of the cottage itself, the studio is not an isolated deviation from the earlier building, but a clever act of historic interpretation and synthesis.

Materials and method pay homage to the natural and architectural settings. Scissor-truss leg supports allow the studio to be set against the hillside with minimal intrusion on the site, and the use of natural timber on the studio structure and bridge allow each to blend with the green surroundings. Meanwhile, a subtle geometric pattern typical of 1920s building design in the region ties the new building firmly to the existing cottage. The studio's exposed structural elements reflect 'the robust character of these early houses'.

The curved copper roof with projecting copper hood is reminiscent of the cottage's outline but affirms the pavilion's debt to contemporary Australian design in one nicely arched stroke. The whole structure – scissor-legs and all – may bring to mind traditional lifeguard towers, but the studio's warm wood interior and view of the Pacific Ocean through native banksia trees would make it difficult for any lifeguard stationed here to leave in a hurry.

sketch

side elevation

[left] The sketch and elevation show the scissor-leg truss supports capped by the angle of the cantilevered roof and the walkway that connects the studio to the main house.
[below and opposite] The studio is clad in black-painted plywood, a reference to the existing house's walls. Windows in the wood interior look out to the Pacific and Palm Beach through verdant native vegetation.

On the banks of the Mondsee near Guglhupf Hill, Hans Peter Wörndl built a cubist construction of plywood panels that is all about movement. Designed as part of the Upper Austrian 'Festival of the Regions', which encouraged the erection of cultural, artistic and architectural objects around the region, 'GucklHupf' is a calm haven and a question mark in the landscape. Described as adhering to the principles of 'movable furniture and the mobile home', the hut makes use of shifting planes to allow the inhabitants to change, modify or eliminate views and light according to their needs. Though it is sympathetically faced in timber, the construction stands out as a visitor on the green site so that the tension between 'strange and familiar, quiet and movement, living and travelling, home and away from home' are expressed in response to the festival's theme, 'Strange(r)'.

Definitions are as flexible as the turning, folding and tilting planes in this design, whose name derives from Gucklhupf, an Austrian cake usually eaten on Sundays, and Guglhupf, the name of the hill on which it was sited. The architect also refers to the verbs gucken, meaning to watch or observe, and hüpfen, to hop, so that the building also represents the idea of 'hopping up and down in an attempt to find a better vantage point', only in this case it is a matter of opening and closing. As the GucklHupf was built by Wörndl and two colleagues on site, it evolved during construction and is intended to 'remain in a state of permanent transformation', as 'a metaphor for travel'. It is perhaps fitting then that, denied permission to remain on the site, the GucklHupf now lies dismantled waiting to behold pastures new.

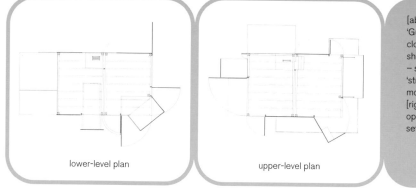

lower-level plan

upper-level plan

[above] The changing face of the 'GucklHupf'. Sliding, opening and closing panels allow for a range of shapes and views – expressions, even – signifying the tension between 'strange and familiar, quiet and movement, living and travelling'.
[right] Different panels of the cube open out to take in the wooded setting or the lake view.

In one sense the GucklHupf is a simple wooden cube with lots of quirky openings; in another it is an exercise in ambiguity positioned somewhere between architecture and sculpture and teasingly hovering outside regional building traditions.

out of the blue

'Point Lookout' Observation Tower
Portable
Richard Horden

Richard Horden and his team of students in Munich have achieved a remarkable feat of compact, holistic architecture. They have addressed the needs of sea observation and of lifeguards who traditionally spend their time in somewhat bulkier wooden towers. After studying rescue stations used on the Bavarian mountain lakes, the Horden team developed 'Point Lookout', a portable observation structure. Here again they exploit the structural and lightweight properties of aluminium to create an object that is adaptable and fully portable.

Like previous Horden designs, Point Lookout uses lengths of aluminium for support and borrows from techniques used in boat construction for simple connections and a slender, graceful profile. Also, the legs are the usual Horden tripod of strength. The whole structure can be broken down into manageable components and with an entire weight of only 70 kilograms, it can all be packed into two bags and carried by as few as two people to locations as inhospitable as the Arctic or as well-travelled as the California coast.

The easily assembled unit consists of a raised platform and shade canopy with an 'integral high-level tent' that can be used as a bivouac in remote locations. Large, triangular metal foot plates distribute the weight over soft sand or coral. Horden believes that each project is 'a sensitive investigation of landscaping, space, light, new technologies, fun and function'. Point Lookout certainly speaks to those elements in a way that, like many of his designs, resonates with what is becoming a familiar, though always inspired, eloquence.

[opposite and previous] Point Lookout is designed to be used by explorers, camera crews and rescue teams in remote locations. The 70-kilogram structure can be fully dismantled and fit into two 'ski-type' bags.
[this page] Heights and levels are adjustable with a frame that works like a camera tripod. The fabric is acrylic canvas, and the aluminium supports are coated with heavy duty, marine-quality paint.

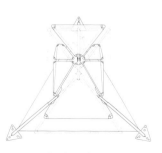

view from above

Horden claims to work 'between', between
traditional architecture and the latest
technology, between earth and sky.

objects in the landscape

Follies, pavilions and sculptural flourishes in natural settings

A popular adornment on rambling English country estates, where visitors might encounter magical little temples, figurines or enchanted grottoes, the folly was part of a general belief that nature was there for man to tame and control, to manipulate to his own designs – even, ironically enough, when those designs were created to enhance the enjoyment of the natural surroundings. Despite their function as symbols of power or control, follies were objects of whimsy and curiosity. And although they served no genuine purpose, their ability to delight and to astound is and was to do with pervading romantic notions about the natural landscape.

Modern-day follies have a wider aim. With an ever-increasing desire to embrace rather than dominate the environment and its forms, the concept of a purposeless or unmeaningful structure is almost anathema to contemporary architects. Asked to create objects in landscape settings, designers seek to impart gravitas to their buildings to shake off the excesses of bygone times. Nowadays, architects pose questions that are more difficult to answer: what is ultimately our relationship to the land and what do our buildings mean within it?

The Copenhagen Architecture Park gives expression to this questioning in schemes by a number of highly respected international architects, all of whom responded to the request to create structures that were in keeping with the vernacular idea of the Danish Garden Colony House, which began life as an unglorious allotment shed at the end of the last century and has now become the latest in high design.

What unites all the structures in this section is their tendency toward becoming sculptural objects, despite the fact that most were built with a specific purpose in mind. Indeed, many are deliberately referential, not in the pastiche postmodern manner of stylized historic detailing but in questioning or distortion of original forms. The park lodges built by MVRDV in the Netherlands, for example, marry the idyllic hut form with its logical semi-urban site: the public park. Here, mythic origin combines with function to provide sensible and sensitive housing for public amenities. When the work day is over and the lodges are closed up, they become sculpture rather than shelter, highlighting the division and overlap of attributes.

Allied Works' Maryhill Overlook is situated on a hillside on the Columbia River Gorge, a beautiful but stark setting. Here, bold concrete slabs are in direct confrontation with nature, establishing a deliberate dialogue between the built and unbuilt environment. Although they share a sculptural disposition with the Maryhill Overlook, Dan Hoffman's community mailbox enclosure and storytelling pavilion engage their surroundings rather than challenge them. Through the use of natural and local materials, they harmonize built form with the natural setting, becoming objects of minimal shelter and pleasant wonder. Thomas Heatherwick's 'Hairy Sitooterie', which is in fact composed of a perfect cube punctured with wood staves, toys with our notion of tactility and scale: from afar the structure seems fluffy, soft to the touch; up close, it appears more aggressive, a guinea pig turned porcupine. From either perspective, this clever manipulation of material with an open, natural presentation forces us to reconsider ideas of function and size within the natural and man-made worlds.

Although architect Hiroshi Nakao's 'Black Maria' and 'Gisant/Transi' structures are probably the most follylike in their immediate appearance — they only provide slight shelter and can be moved to the best siting — they pose a fundamental question for architecture: at what point does a building stop being shelter, functional, and at what point does it become art, an object intended purely for enjoyment, edification or self-awareness? In their own ways, each of these buildings combines a use with a sculptural presence, but whereas follies of old symbolize man's mastery of land or social status, these little objects of architecture bespeak something more profound: a celebration of what is ultimately the most natural act of all, human creativity.

theme park

Park Lodges
Hoge Veluewe Park, The Netherlands
MVRDV

A walk in the park isn't what it used to be at Hoge Veluwe National Park in the Netherlands – it's an architectural experience. Dutch firm MVRDV's competition-winning schemes for three porters' lodges at the park's main entrances make visitors aware that nature is only part of the attraction here. With the Kröller-Müller Museum designed by Henry van de Velde and Sint Hubertus Castle by Hendrik Berlage on the grounds, the architects sought to make the lodges representative of the park's natural and man-made wonders.

Each lodge is made from a material that is directly correlated to the essential features of the site. The structure at the entrance in the village of Rijzenburg, for example, is the most traditional, with an exterior of red cedar that reflects the wooded environment. The Otterlo lodge pays homage to architecture and building with its brick and concrete construction, while the most contemporary building, the Hoenderloo lodge, is made of Cor-Ten steel, which the architects employed as a reference to the modern art in the Kröller-Müller's collection. All three structures are composed entirely of their specified material and can be completely closed up to become sculptural objects in the landscape.

The irregular geometry that inspired this sculptural quality was achieved by starting with the shape of 'the archetypal lodge, the little house', and then skewing it to meet the demands of the site, for example traffic or nearby car parks. Each form is then further distorted so that it appears to be stretching in greeting toward incoming visitors. It is only when each sculpture's 'flaps' are opened to expose information windows that the true nature of MVRDV's 'mysterious objects' is revealed.

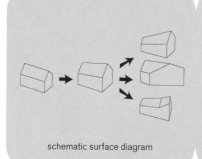

schematic surface diagram

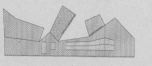

[above] The architecture of the historic
buildings in the park is reflected in
Otterlo lodge's brick and concrete
construction; while [opposite] the
Hoenderloo and Rijzenburg lodges,
respectively, refer to modern art,
through the use of steel, and the
natural setting, through wood.
[far left] The derivation of the forms
begins with a conventional house
before being distorted.
[left] Each lodge can be 'unfolded'
into a two-dimensional plane.

The lodges' shapes evolved from 'the archetypal small house', but the structures become sculptural when closed up. Each being made from a single material, they become pure objects in the landscape.

post modern

Community Mailbox Enclosure
Cranbrook, USA
Dan Hoffman

The American mailbox has not yet gained status as a design icon. But if Dan Hoffman's community mailbox enclosure, designed and built for the Cranbrook Academy campus, is anything to go by, this is not a long-lasting state of affairs.

The Cranbrook Academy in Michigan is legendary as a seat of design inspiration and instruction. The original art school was founded just after the turn of the century by George Booth, publisher of the *Detroit News* newspaper, who was heavily influenced by the Arts and Crafts movement. By the 1920s, Cranbrook came to bear the indelible marks of Finnish designer Eliel Saarinen who graced the campus for twenty-five years with his own designs more tuned to innovation than stylistic definition.

Now, the Cranbrook Academy encompasses a primary and secondary school as well as an Institute of Science and Arts academy. Dan Hoffman became head of the architecture department in 1986, working with his students to, as he says 're-establish the importance of the building arts in architecture'. In 1994 Hoffman and a group of Cranbrook graduates formed a 'design and build studio' called the Cranbrook Architecture Office to work on projects around the campus. Among the works executed by the studio were a new entrance, or gatehouse, a number of bridges, site lighting, signs and exhibits. 'Sometimes our work began with a simple request from the Cranbrook community,' Hoffman explains. Traditionally, especially in rural communities, mailboxes are placed along a roadside at the edge of a property. To provide sheltered access as well as privacy for a group of mailboxes, Hoffman designed the box-shaped pavilion of rough-sawn cedar latticework and seamed copper roof. Here people could have protection from the elements and a pleasant place to chat with the neighbours.

The openwork of the walls lets in natural light while shielding the mailboxes from public view. The effect is a lightly dappled interior that will encourages people to spend much more time getting their mail. And the humble mailbox might find itself the focus of a lot more attention.

[previous] The mailbox enclosure retains a position close to the road for access, but shelters the mailboxes in a light, inviting folly-like structure. [opposite and above] The rough-sawn cedar slats provide a sturdy, protective pavilion that still allows abundant light to the interior.

In the Cranbrook tradition of innovative yet lasting design, Hoffman has installed a new structure, an enclosure for the community's mailboxes, that adds the benefits of both shelter and transparency.

boxed in

Architecture Park
Copenhagen, Denmark
Various Architects

At the end of the nineteenth century, the Danish government leased parcels of land outside Copenhagen as garden or park allotments. Factory workers and other city dwellers had the opportunity to exchange their crowded urban conditions for green subdivisions, each with its own temporary shelter or shed, in the *Kolonihaven*, or 'garden colony'. Through years of use and decoration the sheds have evolved into symbols of individual expression and of the garden colony ideal.

To mark Copenhagen's year as European Capital in 1996, a group of internationally renowned architects were invited to reinterpret the beloved *kolonihavehus* ('garden colony house') for Copenhagen's first architecture park,

by Danish-born architect Kirsten Kiser. Though the *kolonihavehus* is a cherished form of Danish vernacular, Kiser broke with tradition by enjoining a broad spectrum of architects to produce designs for a typical 6-square-metre structure, to be set in an old orchard in Vallensbaek, about forty minutes south of Copenhagen.

The results signal a new global chapter in the story of the humble Danish shed: French architect Dominique Perrault enclosed a tree in four glass walls. Finnish studio Heikkinen-Komonen produced a boxy structure with two levels, white upon black, highlighting darkness and light. Josef Paul Kleihues took the box form to its logical conclusion in his perfect eight-foot cube. Richard Meier's cube sits on a grid with a sliding panel that articulates indoors and out. Alvaro Siza, Aldo Rossi, Michael Graves and Leon Krier all played with the idea of houses in miniature with Leon Krier's thatched cottage slightly reminiscent of something made of gingerbread. Hut evolved to tower in Ralph Erskine's slatted construction, and in Henning Larsen and Arata Isozaki's elevated forms on stilts, while the question of form becomes an exploration in dynamism with Enric Miralles's colliding shapes. The most notable deviation on all fronts is Richard Rogers's transparent pod, which resembles more space station than hut, and which, in keeping with its utter adaptability, could look out of place almost anywhere.

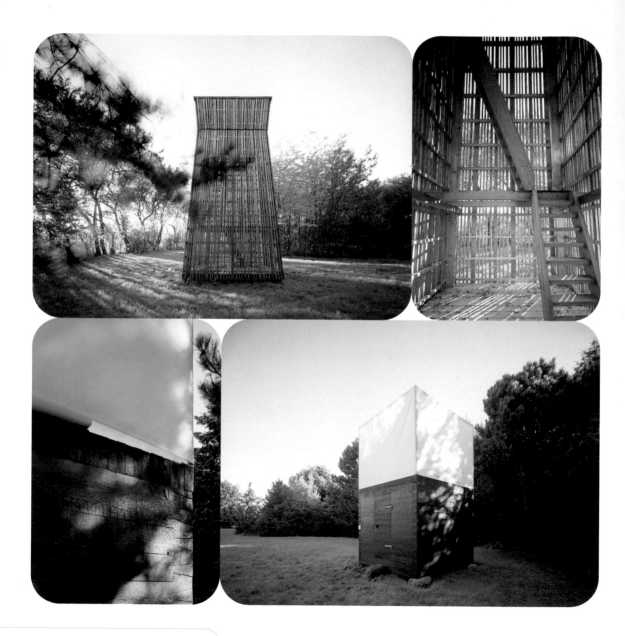

objects in the landscape

[previous page] A man's shed is his castle, especially in the case of Mario Botta's spiky-topped platform, with sticks recalling battlements and a hollow base punctured with tiny peepholes through which to scrutinize unexpected visitors.

[opposite, above] Ralph Erskine's slatted tower is a playful climbing frame, though one that is gracefully tapered and permeated by natural light.

[opposite, below] Mikko Heikkinen and Markku Komonen of Finland made the structure a dialogue of opposites: light versus dark, closed versus open, hard versus soft. The two stacked solid cubes might also refer to earth and sky, with one dark-painted wood box below a roof terrace that has white fabric walls and is open to the sky.

[this page] Dominique Perrault's glass-walled enclosure can be transparent or opaque depending on the desired effect. The plot and tree inside represent the ownership of land, yet it might also be perceived as nature enshrined, an appreciation of the woodland setting itself, rather than humans building within it.

lift off

School Bus Stop
Idaho, USA
Michael Culpepper and Greg Tew

Moscow is not a place you want to be stuck waiting for a bus in the winter, even if it is the town in rural Idaho and not the Russian capital. On a steep site with views across rolling hills at the foot of Moscow Mountain, two Seattle architects constructed a bus shelter for schoolchildren, a welcome retreat during the harsh winters. Its pleasant simplicity of form and function is an exercise in economy of design and materials. The shelter's bulging shape, which the architects refer to as an 'impregnated vessel', is essentially a curved plywood box faced in heavy-gauge sheet aluminium that has been overlapped like shingles. Viewed from the road or surrounding woods, the bus shelter looks more like a high-tech tent for futuristic campers than a secured, permanent structure.

Each side of the building was cut from a single sheet of curved 6.3-millimetre-thick structural plywood. The sheets were then fixed with screws and brackets, with no additional bracing, so that the exterior also forms the interior (although a vapour barrier between the metal and the wood reduces condensation effects). Inside, childsize seats are attached to stringers that rest on two beams and step up the hill's slope. The beams themselves are attached to concrete pilings, allowing the enclosed skin to appear to be hovering over the site.

The entire assembly was completed off site, 'using techniques more akin to furniture making – moulded plywood and structural skin – than architecture', which attests to the compact and portable nature of this innovative structure. Described as something 'half spaceship–half fish' because of its silvery scaley appearance, the project was viewed by the architects as 'a vehicle to study form in the landscape', the difficult terrain and concise structure being an inspiration for 'unusual construction methods'.

The first schoolchildren to arrive at the finished shelter gave it unanimous high marks, calling it 'cool' and 'awesome', an enthusiastic reception that should appeal to architects from Idaho to Siberia.

[opposite] The shiny sheet-aluminium shingle skin and missile shape answer demanding site and temperature requirements.
[above] The structural skin is composed of bent plywood, with each side cut from a single sheet of three layers that have been glued, screwed and clamped together.
[below] The drawings show how the structure steps up the hillside.

'When the school bus pulled up to the shelter for the first time, one December afternoon, the kids sat up, leaned towards one side of the bus and quickly wiped the condensation off the windows to get a better view.'

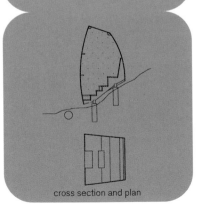

cross section and plan

desert flowering

Maryhill Nature Overlook
Washington, USA
Allied Works Architects

A concrete Greek key unfolding over the arid terrain of the Columbia River Gorge, the Maryhill Overlook cuts a distinctive divide across an undeveloped landscape. Rather than functioning as a physical blockade, however, the viewing platforms manifest the idea of boundaries, for the perpendicular planes of concrete encourage more interaction than they prevent. Boundaries here have more to do with aesthetic divisions between art and architecture, between building and sculpture, between natural and man-made. The physical object itself suggests more openness than closure and generously allows the visitor to perceive the setting around and

through it rather than forcing concentration on the space within it or the structure itself.

Maryhill Overlook is the first in a series of 'sitings', a concept developed by Brad Cloepfil, principal of Allied Works, with his architecture students at the University of Oregon. The idea was to erect 'small buildings or rooms' on five sites in the United States' Pacific Northwest region which were chosen to display the built and unbuilt environments typical of the region. In addition to Columbia Gorge, a high desert site, there are constructions in forested, agricultural, suburban and urban settings.

The Maryhill Art Museum commissioned Allied Works to build one of these sitings on an undetermined place within its 2,400 hectares of land; funding came from state, local and federal agencies. Views in and around the overlook take in dramatic columnar basalt cliffs, as well as the eerie treeless landscape that stretches toward the 2,400-metre volcanic peaks of the Cascade Mountains. Nine concrete slabs and eight walls 'provide varying degrees of exposure to and protection from the elements'. Emerging from the landscape as a bold tectonic with its own calligraphy, this robust and challenging form is a far cry from the follies perched in romantic manicured English gardens, a difference that represents perhaps the greatest divide of all.

cross sections

plan and longitudinal section

[above] Unfolding on an arid bluff above the Columbia River Gorge, the enigmatic form is enhanced against the surreal high-desert landscape. [opposite] The plan and sections show the configurations of the nine concrete slabs and eight concrete walls. The uppermost level extends from a large shelf of land, with subsequent levels occurring at different elevations relative to the sloping site.

'From some vantage points a sense of habitable space is created, yet from others the construction almost disappears into the landscape beyond … creating boundaries and apertures for space and light in a virtually boundless landscape.'

full circle

Storytelling Pavilion
Cranbrook, USA
Dan Hoffman

Now dubbed 'Pickle Place' by the children who make use of its magical ambience, Dan Hoffman's storytelling pavilion is one of numerous projects executed under the Cranbrook Architecture Office formed by Hoffman and Cranbrook Academy graduates. Set on a small island in a stream that runs alongside the Brookside School at Cranbrook, the pavilion was built to compensate for the fact that the former riverside storytelling spot had been paved over by development. To continue the tradition of using the stream as a storytime setting, Hoffman designed the pavilion to take in the vista of the water through an open-ended shape but also to block out the view of the new parking lot. The island is accessed by a specially designed bridge, also by Hoffman.

In response to the legend of a battle that took place between a local native American tribe and European settlers at a nearby site, Hoffman wanted to 'evoke the memory of the native peoples', as 'the legacy of the European settlers was already well represented' by the existing school buildings. Carved-wood poles wrapped in cedar-shake tiles contribute to a structure that conjures the native American teepee and adds the tantalizing air of legend to the already picturesque site.

This is not the only time Dan Hoffman has turned his attention toward the children of Cranbrook: his designs for bentwood furniture for the local kindergarten make use of methods of working with moulded plywood that Charles Eames developed with Eliel's son Eero Saarinen while both were at Cranbrook. It seems fitting that it is now time for another legacy, artistic rather than warlike, to haunt this part of Michigan.

[previous page] The storytelling pavilion, nicknamed 'Pickle Place' by local schoolchildren, is set on a small island within a stream; a bridge provides access.
[above] The design of pole and cedar-shingle recalls native American structures, a reference to the history of the area.

Teachers from the local school have traditionally used the banks of the stream as a place for study and recreation, as well as for storytelling.

mysterious strangers

'Black Maria' and 'Gisant/Transi' Mobile Pavilions
Portable
Hiroshi Nakao

Adaptable architecture or poseable sculpture? Japanese architect Hiroshi Nakao's experiments with light, form, space and movement seem to hover on the convergence of many paths – and that is just what he intends.

With a limited palette of materials – black-stained plywood, ash, concrete and steel – he has created a pair of structures that pose more questions than they answer. 'Black Maria' is a series of rectangular walls on steel wheels that could be mistaken for mobile packing crates or a portable theatrical backdrop, but behind the walls a hollow rectangle forms a platform hemmed in by vertical steel rods. The platform and the rods seem to beckon visitors inside, to walk through the narrow and strangely open but subtly articulated space.

On closer inspection the walls' curvature is more apparent, as is the structure's flexibility. Walls can be drawn together to form a dark, closed hollow or opened so that the hollow 'folds back on itself, like a glove turned inside out'. 'Black Maria' was the nickname given to the film studio built for Edison's Kinetoscope, which allowed moving pictures to be viewed through a peephole. It is the idea of a hole of light providing a wider vision that Nakao seized upon. 'Black Maria' has particular similarities with the dilation and contraction of the camera eye, the restriction and abundance of light.

If 'Black Maria' is about the manipulation of space around light, 'Gisant/Transi' brings the focus into the dark. The name refers to a kind of tomb art that appeared in Europe in the wake of the Black Death and depicted the

deceased as both dead 'transi' and living 'gisant'. With narrow sightlines punctuated by steel bars and hard slabs long enough to lie upon, Nakao's forms in concrete and steel unnervingly recall the tombs.

Both structures invite the observer to step inside and to peer out through the bars or the boxed openings. Again, the elements can be reconfigured for closure or openness and the visitor left wondering at – and encouraged to view – all the angles, while pondering the nature of inside and out, light and dark, life and death.

[previous page and right] The concrete-and-wood 'Gisant/Transi' explores ideas of openness and closure. Its platforms are wide enough for a body to lie down for a 'night of half-sleep'.
[opposite] 'Black Maria' is an experiment in light. Inspired by the Kinetoscope, an early device for watching motion pictures, Nakao's construction is primarily a tool for viewing.
[below and opposite, above] The drawings show the graphic quality of the movable pieces and their multiple arrangements.

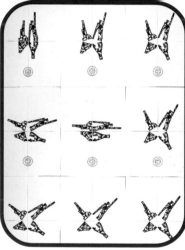

From the concep-
tion of 'the interior
space, the nature
of its boundaries
and the play of
light within', the
architect was
concerned with
'creating hollows',
a deliberately
ambiguous
spatial condition.

hairy house

'Sitooterie' Gazebo
Northumberland, England
Thomas Heatherwick

From a distance you might think a curiously large hedgehog was sunning itself on the lawn, but on closer inspection you would discover the curiously textural creation of Thomas Heatherwick. Invited along with eleven other architects and designers to produce a place for quiet contemplation for the gardens of Belzay Estate in Northumberland, Heatherwick responded with true aplomb. English Heritage sponsored this celebration of the 'sitooterie', a Scottish term meaning, literally, 'sit-outerie' that suggests something akin to a gazebo or folly. Heatherwick jumped at the commission as an opportunity to experiment on a small scale with the idea of giving a building a tactile quality. 'I was interested in the texture of buildings, how they might be different shapes, some are curvy or straight, but texture is usually hard-edged,' he explains.

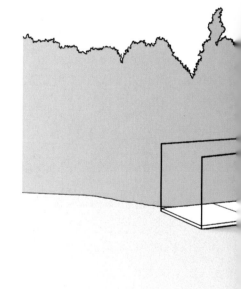

So he made a perfect cube of plywood painted blue and then pierced the volume with 5,100 ash staves that are a metre long and 90 millimetres square. The staves serve a range of functions besides giving the building its prickly appearance. Those on the bottom actually support the structure and make for a springy floor, which is another aspect of the building that Heatherwick finds fascinating: 'It's a structure that weighs four tonnes and is supported by stakes that you can break with your hands.' The staves also provide interior texture, since Heatherwick also has a penchant for what he calls 'seeing things through.' The staves penetrate the interior by about 5 millimetres, providing the textural equivalent of

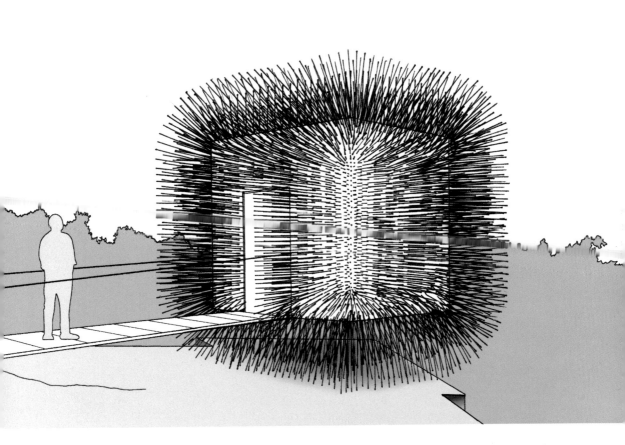

'spotty wallpaper'. In some places where seating was needed, the staves come through far enough to support benches (the Hairy Sitooterie can seat up to eight people), becoming once again part of the structure.

In this way, the exterior becomes interior, something that also appeals to the designer, as does the profile of the exterior which rather than showing a sharp division between the object and its setting, presents a rather blurred division of the two. Looking at it on the horizon, Heatherwick says, 'I like that you can't tell where the building ends and the sky begins', and not the slightest mention of hedgehogs.

'I was hoping a bird would come along and nest in it,' says Heatherwick, 'but we must have missed nesting season.'

Over 5,000 metre-long ash staves inserted into the core cube serve a multiplicity of functions and add an air of whimsy to the structure. They support an interior bench, provide textured interior walls and give the whole building spring support, endowing it with physical as well as visual movement.

furnishing the city

Innovative utilitarian structures that adorn our streets and daily lives

As much as the urban experience is determined by grand tributes to art, culture and government, it is the smaller, utilitarian structures of everyday existence that can provide the most unexpected delights. Here micro-architecture is not so much about whimsy or experiment as about necessity. The architectural objects that make a city function and that nearly every inhabitant uses or comes into contact with impart, and in some ways help to determine, the character of cities around the world. The aesthetic appeal of a transportation system, for example, affects commuters and tourists just as much as its efficiency. Most people have instant associations with the Art Nouveau signage for the Paris Métro or London's bright red phone boxes or classic underground map. Given the impact of street furniture on the individual user, it is hard to believe that the vast majority of these structures are drab and uninspired. The hard facts of urban conditions too often lead to a determinism that allows mediocre design to pass for the best we can expect.

Still, while usefulness and robustness are preconditions for the structures used for bus shelters, public lavatories or train stations, those qualities need not be harbingers of architectural doom. High-tech materials and thoughtful design can combat vandalism and weathering while providing shelter or function. The challenge, it seems, is to shed our preconceived notions of what street furniture should look like and explore what it can look like and how it might be used differently while performing under the tough demands of city life.

The structures included here are exceptional in how they contribute to the cityscape in small but very perceptible ways. For instance, although advances in self-cleaning, automated flushing and tap flow make the maintenance of some public toilets more manageable, introducing such buildings as objects of innovative and creative thinking is still an anomaly. We may not wish to celebrate the function of these facilities, but we can work to achieve higher aesthetic, as well as utilitarian, standards.

When a building for a new public toilet was proposed in west London and a neighbourhood group objected to its design, CZWG Architects were called in. By rethinking the entire pedestrian area in which the facility would be placed, instead of just concentrating on the loos, they addressed local concerns and included trees, bicycle racks and benches in their scheme, as well as new parking arrangements and a flower kiosk. Also thinking beyond the brief, the landscape architecture and urban planning firm West 8 redesigned a market square in Rotterdam to resolve problems of space and power supplies to the vendors. Revitalizing the square as a public meeting place, complete with electrical 'trees' as power points, proved a significant benefit.

Since transportation is a lifeline to the city, any improvement is bound to have an effect greater than its original purpose. Martin Despang's Hanover metro stops bring uniquely referential design to each of thirteen platforms, each featuring a different material and detailing. Peter Eisenman's anti–bus stop in Aachen, Germany, reinstates the generous seating and shelter that have been slowly chipped away by recent urban design practices. For a bus shelter that can be reconfigured to become a coffee kiosk, bicycle shed or information kiosk for a university campus in northern California, Wes Jones drew on classic regional designs while reimagining functional pieces as adaptable units that provide a range of uses.

Given its fragility, glass is not generally used for urban furniture, but Carlos Zapata and Jörg Joppien did so with deliberate intent. The glass planes of Zapata's Miami gateway enhance the sensation of light and transparency in a sunny seaside city. Joppien's Frankfurt newspaper kiosk is a glass cube by day and an impregnable steel-grid panelled cage at night; both objects exuding much more than utilitarian character. In so far as function can be articulated by material, Shuhei Endo transmuted hardy corrugated steel into the soft curves of a small train station in Japan's Fukui prefecture, a perfect example of how such design can 'bring people together'.

ship shape

Gateway Structure
Miami Beach, USA
Wood and Zapata

Every big city has its heyday and Miami Beach has had a few. Having become synonymous with pastel-shaded Art Deco, the resort boasts layers of a more sophisticated architectural heritage that encompass not just buildings but street furniture, shelters and pedestrian areas. In their three-year restoration project focusing on Lincoln Road and its pedestrian mall, which had suffered decades of neglect and fallen into almost complete disrepair, the Boston architectural firm of Wood and Zapata responded to the influential work of Miami Beach architect Morris Lapidus, who laid out shelters and plantings along the road in the 1960s. As the final element of the area's renewal, the gateway functions as a centre for visitor information.

The pavilion is made up of vertical planes of glass topped by a steel and aluminium roof. Supported by columns and stabilized by tensor cables, the roof recalls the form of a tautly stretched sail, in keeping with the historic seaside setting. Despite the solidity achieved by such firm anchorage, the cantilevered roof and shardlike glass sections cohere in an extremely pleasant, slight but dynamic profile of a body in motion.

Set between two rectangular pools, with one glass wall rising up directly from the water, the form also brings to mind a great winged seabird or a speed boat cutting through the ocean. As such, it is a structure that is rich with allusions and yet devoid of weighty architectural reminders, a floating, gliding prism inviting views of Miami's colourful past and glistening future.

The fact that this is part of a scheme to restore an area once known for its cohesive plan, which included decorative elements along its pedestrian zones, suggests that looking back before going forward can be an educational and surprisingly liberating practice for urban designers.

[right] With all the tapering lines of a racing yacht, the structure tilts forward, while interior cables and columns anchor the structure earthward. Pools of water play off the dramatically cantilevered roof.

[below] The computer model and plans demonstrate the dynamism of the colliding planes against the pools. Glass and aluminium elements emphasize transparency and natural light.

computer renderings

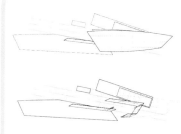

roof and floor plans

Functional, linear, durable – rarely do train stations in outlying suburbs exhibit imagination or finesse. Enter Shuhei Endo and his constructions of corrugated steel. Like some kind of balloon sculptor twisting logical shapes from unlikely beginnings, Endo has stretched an industrial material and the commuter mind to new dimensions.

The site, a former railroad siding, is narrow and spectacularly linear with houses lining one side and paddy fields along the other. The structure had to offer sheltered waiting areas and bicycle storage, and the skin, ranging in thickness from 2.7 to 7 millimetres, needed to withstand heavy snow. It seemed an appropriate project for the material that Endo has previously and successfully alchemized into such distinctive forms.

In this plan the architect limited himself to three basic forms: a simple cantilever with one side of the steel plate

anchored to the ground; a gate-shaped frame that is attached to the cantilever; and a continuous plate that is almost bent double and anchored on both sides. Arranged in a varied pattern, the combinations of these three 'types' produce a succession of wave-like curves that wake the sleepy plane. A robust and pliable material that is widely used in such broad contexts as train stations, warehouses, factories and farms for its strength and durability, corrugated steel has obvious practical advantages, but Endo's transformation goes further than function to promote the unmanned station as 'a centre for communal exchanges', to encourage contact among passengers. Using the 'long corridor as an open gallery' the demarcations between roof and wall, interior and exterior dissolve, and a greater degree of openness and accessibility to the public is readily achieved.

The veritable playground of curves imparts a light and user-friendly quality to the industrial material while providing all the practical advantages.

[opposite and above] The unmanned train station welcomes passengers with a succession of curving metal sheets that provide shelter and openness. Space for sheltered bicycle storage is also provided within the curving forms.

[right] Endo began with a sine wave, taking sections as models for his curves which are used in three basic derivations.

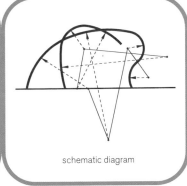

schematic diagram

variations on the three forms

bodies electric

Electricity Masts
Rotterdam, The Netherlands
West 8

Street markets and public squares are an integral, if semi-transient, component of the European urban landscape. The demands of these spaces are quite specific and essentially twofold: to allow space for vendors to erect stalls at least once a week, creating the kind of carnival atmosphere that animates an entire neighbourhood; and to remain somehow appealing on non-market days, managing to look expectant rather than abandoned.

Although the refurbishment of the Visserijplein market square in Rotterdam was requested on a very modest budget, fortunately for the planners and public at large, landscape architects and urban planners West 8 engineered a solution that excelled in creativity and practicality if not in cost.

A neglected square with little public space and narrow paths between cramped stalls that were easy targets for thieves and pickpockets was transformed into an 'intimate terrace for the community' with generous stall areas, wider access, clearly demarcated borders and an extra row of trees. Cars were also banished from the square, adding the feeling if not the reality of more space. But perhaps the most remarkable feature of the revitalizing plan is West 8's solution to the power supplies for individual market stalls. Electrical cabinets were produced as 'surreal steel trees' and placed throughout the square. Despite being made of standard materials and with 'almost no opportunity for detailing' because of budget constraints, the electricity masts are distinctive points of interest in a scheme full of imaginative problem-solving.

The residents now have a defined neighbourhood square; the market vendors have a traditional market with a modern feel and, more importantly, convenient access to necessary power points. But the Visserijplein does more than fulfill the needs of local organizations. However modest in material and detail, the vibrant sculptural electricity masts ensure that even uninhabited, the square is a living public space.

The symbol of landscape architects West 8's redesign of the Visserijplein market square in Rotterdam is the sculptural electricity mast that allows vendors to access power for their stalls at various points around the square.
[left] The revitalized square is now a popular gathering place.
[below] The *vleugel*, or 'wing', form. The masts are 3.1 metres high, and fourteen supply power for 200 market stalls.

Facilities, services, ladies, gents, lavatories, loo — public toilets by any other name seem to conjure a universally malodorous experience of a supremely uninviting urban necessity. Lucinda Lambton has called them 'Temples of Convenience', and architects CZWG have certainly latched on to this more elevated perception in their design of a lavatory building in west London, going so far as to include space for a flower kiosk, a blatant rejection of everything we have come to associate with public toilets.

This grander vision encompassed the rearrangement of the site itself, so that a new triangular island was created and dotted with trees, benches and bicycle stands; an inefficient car park was reorganized in the process. The resulting plan presents a bright face on public amenities — including a large clock — which usually appear as nondescript afterthoughts of urban planning.

The wonderful logic of the arrangement is enhanced by the detailing. Clad in turquoise-glazed brick, the lavatory structure is a smaller triangle set within that of the island. Continuous horizontal louvres line the top of the walls to provide essential ventilation but also to serve as a decorative base for the translucent, fan-shaped roof that recalls the vivid Art Nouveau details of the Paris métro. Plate glass inserted into the glazed-brick plinth at the point of the triangle forms the flower kiosk, where the turquoise makes a striking backdrop for floral displays. Lavatory entrances at the base of the triangle are marked by 'dancing silhouettes' on steel entrance doors. The architects say that the figures 'advertise the building's use … and celebrate the yearly passing carnival', but one is more inclined to see the happy poses as a sign of the joy one must feel in encountering a facility like this during a moment of need.

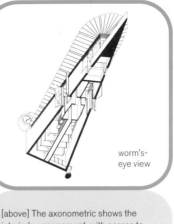

worm's-eye view

[above] The axonometric shows the interior's arrangement, with access to toilets for men and women provided on two sides of the triangular form. The flower kiosk is located at the narrow apex under the fanning roof overhang. [opposite and left] The transparent roof, turquoise enamel tiles, graphic figures and oversize clock make a vivid presence amidst a busy traffic area.

Apart from the other elements that one does not normally associate with structures of this kind, such as the flower kiosk and the use of natural light, there is a dynamism in the design. The bright triangular structure within a triangular area of services causes passersby to stop and take note of this building, whatever its purpose.

grid iron

Newspaper Kiosk
Frankfurt, Germany
Jörg Joppien

It is not uncommon to find temporary structures that are modelled on their more permanent cousins, but it is less common to find designs inspired the other way around. Jörg Joppien's scheme for a newspaper and magazine stand in Frankfurt takes its form from the traditional temporary fruit and vegetable stands located in the nearby Schweizer Platz.

Essentially a glass cube covered with steel-gridded panels, the kiosk addresses security issues while maintaining a pleasing aesthetic presence. The glass cube at the core puts the entire contents of the 5-square-metre premises on display during working hours, but is completely covered by the 'protective skin of movable grid panels' that are attached both vertically and from the roof. The cube's gridded surface is also resistant to graffiti and more destructive forms of vandalism.

When opened, the panels slide, fold and tip to minimize their intrusion in an otherwise highly transparent design. The gridded planes then become a dynamic design feature: vertical panels fold back neatly into the corners like traditional folding screens or shutters, while L-shaped roof-anchored grids swing up to give the kiosk a distinctive profile. The top panels also cantilever beyond the roof to produce a protective overhang for customers and outside display racks. Inside the cube amid the stacks of publications, there is just enough room for a chair and desk for the stallkeeper to operate comfortably.

Compact, sensible and yet delightfully dynamic, this exercise in thoroughly utilitarian urban design will no doubt have lasting appeal and function.

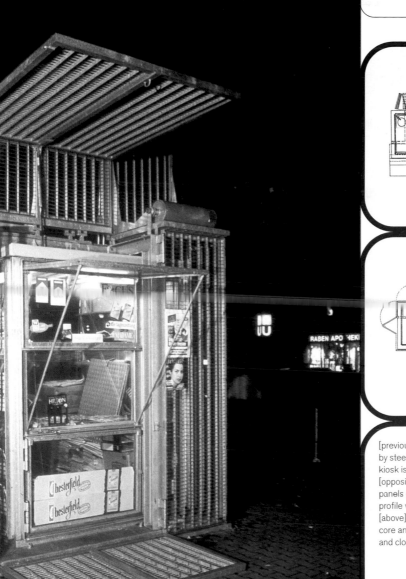

plans

[previous page] Completely enclosed
by steel-gridded protective panels, the
kiosk is resistant to vandalism.
[opposite and left] The hinged rooftop
panels give the kiosk a distinctive
profile when opened.
[above] Plans show the glass cube
core and various positions of the open
and closed panels.

station mastery

Metro Stops
Hanover, Germany
Despang Architekten

'Urban space is not always treated very kindly,' says Martin Despang, who, with his father's firm, won a competition to design thirteen tram platforms and waiting facilities for a new urban rail line serving the EXPO 2000 in Hanover. Yet these graceful steel-framed structures are as kind on the eye as on the traveller, protecting waiting passengers from the road traffic and providing chunky, generous seating. In a 'holistic approach' to the functional, technical and economic parameters, Despang created a system of vertical rectangular blocks that could be covered in a range of materials, and to which could be added the structure's individual 'attire'. In his effort to strike a 'dialogue with the surrounding urban space', Despang conceived different claddings and finishings in response to each facility's immediate surroundings.

At the Haltestelle and Freundallee stops, for example, where brick is the neighbourhood's prevailing building material, the structures are given dry-pressed brick facings; at the Presshaus stop, basalt slabs with glass inlays and panels inscribed with fragments of Kurt Schwitters's 1922 artwork *Z A (Elementar)* pay homage to the artists stint at a nearby publisher. Other 'waiting blocks' feature prepatinated copper (with the ensuing oxidization reflecting the natural evolution of nearby allotments), satin-finished glass blocks, larch strips and stainless-steel mesh and even the now-ubiquitous precast concrete.

To combat the unkind treatment such facilities must endure, Despang was proactive and preventive: all built-in elements, such as information windows, are fitted flush; finishes were treated with lab-tested coatings to protect against weather and graffiti, and the construction makes use of smooth, non-adhesive surfaces to defy would-be vandals. To the waiting passenger, however, the shelters Despang describes as 'urban punctuation' present bold exclamation points of pleasant surprise.

[previous pages] The Kronsberg stop features stone cladding reminiscent of the old village nearby. The glass cladding of the Krügerskamp stop is occasionally filled with 'a mist-like vapour' as part of an art installation. At the Bult stop satin-finished glass blocks were used.
[opposite] Unique detailing gives each block individual character.
[below] The six variations used at each stop incorporate elements for display, seating and standing.

The repeated blocks made use of modular efficiency, while site-specific detailing at each stop conveys the luxury of unique design.

diagrams showing variable elements

assembly required

Modular Shelters
Stanford, USA
Jones, Partners: Architecture

It's a coffee kiosk, a bus shelter, a bicycle rack, a mechanical screen. Wes Jones's 'flexible kiosk prototype' grew out of a brief to design a coffee stand for Stanford University, an institution Jones describes as 'consistently vested in classicism', and expanded as much in style as in the range of its functions.

At first sight the finished design may not appear to be rooted in the campus vernacular, although the trellis roof section is a faint allusion to the particular brand of northern California Spanish Colonial style pioneered by Bernard Maybeck. Perhaps it is the campus's heritage combined with the kiosk's muscular modular versatility that makes Jones's system so remarkable. The thick columns' profiles and the low-pitched roof, rendered in painted steel and site-cast concrete, might have been traced over the template of the adobe-esque or wood-framed precursors around the campus.

By varying the use and number of standardized roof, column and screen elements, the structure is thoroughly flexible, ensuring that no single style is severely adhered to. The bus shelter's raised-angle roof bears less resemblance to California Mission style than the plan for the bike shelter, in which the pitched roof is inverted to produce a valley running lengthwise between two projecting wings. The coffee kiosk contains a bench and counter, as well as the coffee vendor's 'production module'. The bicycle shelter sports a double row of columns with racks between; the mechanical screen variation presents a single row of five columns, a single eave of roof and screens between the bays. The bus shelter is the most pared down of the forms, comprising two columns that support the roof's flying framework.

In his creation of a prototype for other structures, Jones's feat of architectural origami derives from the primitive hut form. Rather than performing a simple variation of forms, however, Jones explains that using the hut as a model permits an 'interpretation of an imagined ideal … So each rediscovery is actually an invention, holding a mirror up to the discoverer.' Complex ideas expressed in simple and, better yet, beautifully functional and multipliable forms.

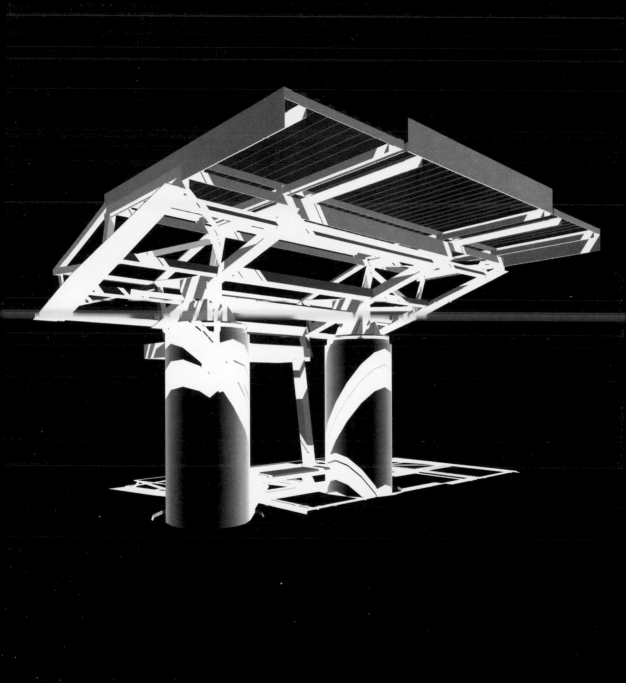

bike rack: elevation

bus shelter: elevation

coffee kiosk: elevation

bike rack: section

bus shelter: section

coffee kiosk: section

bike rack: perspective

bus shelter: perspective

coffee kiosk: perspective

Design and assembly adapt to any of four structural units: bus shelter, coffee kiosk, bicycle rack and mechanical screen. The pitched roof pays homage (at varying angles) to the Mission-style architecture of California. A variety of arrangements of the classically derived columns allow for versatility in function, with each 'bay' capable of taking on inserted racks, screens or enclosures.

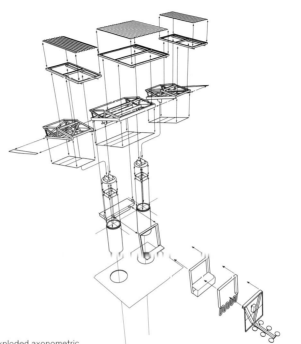

exploded axonometric

roof detail

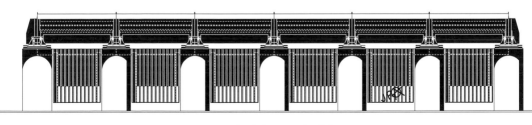

mechanical screen: elevation

Modular Shelters

angle pose

Bus Shelter
Aachen, Germany
Eisenman Architects

Peter Eisenman is known as much for deconstructing as constructing, so it is no surprise that his design for a bus shelter calls into question the conventional ideas of shelter, indeed of the whereabouts of buses. Set several metres from the curbside in the middle of Aachen's central plaza, it might seem that even the buses are to be put off by Eisenman's particular and contrary vision. Yet, since urban street furniture is often designed to resist destruction, one cannot help but welcome structures that dare to offer ample shelter and seating in conjunction with innovative design. In that context, Peter Eisenman was the right choice to redesign the bus shelter for the design-minded, especially since the project was commissioned by JC Decaux, a French company that specializes in street furniture manufacture.

This structure's insectoidal form is the result of a series of triangular planes placed at increasingly wide (or narrowing) angles. The 'feet' of the shelter are formed by the wide end of vertical triangles, though no two are alike and the whole is a play of surfaces, angles and perspectives. As one moves through the building, faceted planes shift before the eye as in a drawing by

M.C. Escher. The two-tone grey-and-gold finish suggests a sort of interior-exterior dialogue, except that the grey often peers from beneath the gold, like bits of handkerchief that refuse to stay tucked inside the breast pocket. Glass panes inserted into the roof and broad

benches formed by the upfold of the grey planes make this a very civilized spot for waiting or just taking umbrage from the elements.

Separate from the shelter but integral to the scheme is an electronic billboard that displays the time and local city information, as if in this context providing mere bus schedules would be outré. With the billboard giving the distinct impression of a raised head, Eisenman's animate form looks very likely to run away just when you've settled in.

The twisting planes are reminiscent of brain-teasing, three-dimensional geometric puzzles. One suspects that somehow it could all be worked neatly into a cube.

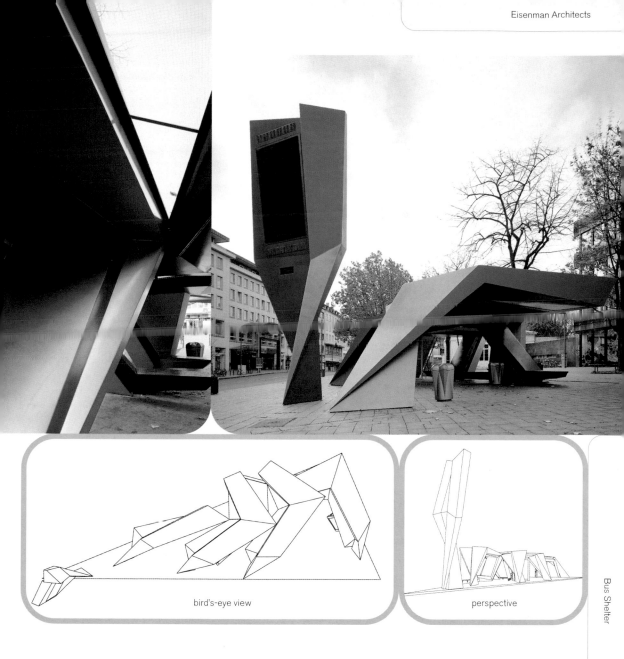

bird's-eye view

perspective

the functional sublime

Celebrating utility through beauty, whether in
an urban or natural environment

Arguments over form versus function are like chicken and egg. What distinguishes these celebrations of functional form or formal function is how they overturn or exceed expectations. It is not uncommon for purely functional buildings of the past to be hailed in later generations as works of grand artistic merit. Factory buildings, for example, once perceived as awkward brick giants have become fashionable venues for restaurants, art museums and loft apartments; the more the vestiges of function can be held intact, the better.

The following examples, however, will not have to wait for appreciation to come through adaptation or creative re-use. These projects reject the notion that function implies a dumbing down of form. By rethinking standard models and minimizing the size or impact of the structure within its physical context, these architects have responded to the challenge of small utilitarian buildings with originality and innovation.

Japanese architect Hitoshi Abe's water tower for Miyagi Prefecture in Japan is one example of how conventional form can be improved to dramatic effect. Since the brief was to make a structure as unintrusive as possible in an undeveloped site, Abe first 'reduced' the height and then covered the building in a steel-mesh 'negligee' to encourage overgrowth, quite a design understatement and a rarity in utilitarian public architecture.

Also faced with the challenge of minimizing the local impact of a tower, Gunnar Birkerts devised a cellular telephone mast that not only bucked the trend for unsightly technical spires but embraced the vertical form as sculpture capable of possessing interest and exuding grace. It now ranks among the Latvian architect's many positive contributions to the architectural landscape of Ann Arbor, Michigan.

Rather than minimizing the spectacle of the public water supply, Brookes Stacey Randall architects created a barometer in London that celebrates it. Their transparent tower enclosing a stainless-steel vertical pipe allows surges in the city's water pressure to be made visible, so that pedestrians and drivers on the London ring road can appreciate function firsthand and admire the creative display of a mostly unrecognized process.

Crafting an inspired structure from a mundane requirement is a shared aim of many architects in this book. In the realm of small, functional buildings it is an especially potent challenge. Whether thinking large or small, however, the architects of the Amsterdam-based UN Studio strongly hold that all public architecture should be a marriage between architects and civil engineers, between art and function, to produce buildings of lasting value. Their bridge and bridge-master's house in Purmerend performs all of the required functions – with a few extra thrown in – while making only a slight impact on the riverfront view.

Shuhei Endo's trademark corrugated-steel curves were put to sculptural and practical use in a lavatory and park-keeper's office for an otherwise nondescript suburban park. Even though in this case the park is a new and not terribly interesting setting, Endo has used the curves of his design to help the structure blend in shape if not in appearance with the grassy hillside and yet gently articulate the areas of use.

Even the humble garden shed can be made over, as demonstrated by Carl-Viggo Hølmebakk's towering reinvention in Oslo. Not content to squeeze a traditional wood box onto a narrow site or to expand the box at the expense of the garden's trees, Hølmebakk directed his gaze upward and devised a circular tower that accommodates storage and workshop space in a highly unusual form for a garden shed that does much more than keep the rain off the lawn mower.

Clearly when architects of such a distinguished calibre undertake the design of functional structures we would expect the results to be noteworthy, even when 'thinking small' is a guiding principle. Yet in the built world at large there are precious few examples that engage in the debate over form versus function and end up enlarging both.

Given a few sheets of corrugated steel and a site to bend them toward, there is little that Shuhei Endo cannot do. What might have been a utilitarian project has become a delicate form in the landscape. In the mountains of Hyogo Prefecture, an hour's train journey from the bustling hub of Osaka, a small park carved out of a meagre space between primary- and secondary- school buildings has the somewhat grander distinction of being home to this wonderfully flowing facility.

Curved structures that give the appearance of curled butter shavings are arranged to encompass three rooms: men's and women's public lavatories and a park-keeper's office. As the sheets of ribbed steel curve and twist, floors become walls, interior becomes exterior and fixed ideas about the division between those elements are called into question. Similarly, the industrial materials themselves, which might seem better suited to an urban setting, successfully blend into the site's close landscaping. Slanted back at a slight angle, the gently sloping curves echo the rolling hillside backdrop.

Described by the architect as 'halftecture' (half+ architecture), the deceptively 'simple arrangement of parts' explores the characteristics of 'openness and closedness'. Derived from shapes cut from a sine wave, the form is distinctly open-ended, 'suggesting the possibility of entrance from almost anywhere', while issues of security and privacy are addressed efficiently through the addition of reinforced auxiliary materials

and the inherent strength of the steel sheeting. In one
fell swoop, Shuhei Endo has bestowed a graceful
dignity upon modest but necessary conveniences in
an otherwise unremarkable park space. In or out, open
or closed, Endo's sinuous shapes are all about
unbounded expectations.

'As a facility for general use', says the architect, 'the park itself defies expression of any regional character'. His undulating design happily fills the void.

[opposite, left] What appears from the outside as sculpture is transformed as enclosure.
[opposite, right] Newly planted trees will help an already surprisingly organic form blend with the park grounds.
[right] The seemingly complex form was generated from a sine curve.
[below] The structure presents a pleasing take on utilitarian facilities in an otherwise unremarkable suburban park outside Osaka.

schematic diagram

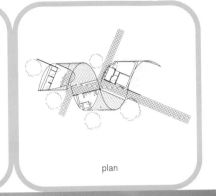

plan

Call them the new telephone poles, but the fact that cellular-phone relay towers are soon to become as ubiquitous as their land-line counterparts is something more than a few people find disturbing. The location is generally decided by the distance required for transmission and does not necessarily coincide with that of other towers, structures or infrastructure, so their appearance on the landscape can be even more startling than a strand of power lines across an undeveloped hillside or along a scenic drive.

Responding to objections to the indiscriminate placement of such towers, the Airtouch company had to look carefully to find a site for their most efficient and productive tower in the university town of Ann Arbor, Michigan. They chose a spot on property belonging to Thomas Monaghan, owner of the Domino's Pizza chain, who agreed to lease a parcel of land near his corporate headquarters on the condition that the tower be 'a memorable sculptural object' and that it be designed by Gunnar Birkerts, the architect responsible for the Domino's complex.

The resulting 'sculpture' takes its form from 'an airborne signal, reaching for the earth with the speed and image of lightning'. Indeed the cobalt-blue tower's lightning-bolt shape is immediately discernible above its 8-metre-deep steel cason. The 50-metre-tall structure is illuminated at night, while the fibre-optic cables change colour during the day to indicate weather conditions. A red cube at the foot of the tower is a steel-clad shelter for electronic equipment; at the top is a 'nest', or cellular platform. Guywires attached at structural joints secure the tower.

As telecommunication become increasingly wireless, clearly the earthbound pole and wire will become a thing of the past as the sculptural weather vanes of the future make their landings.

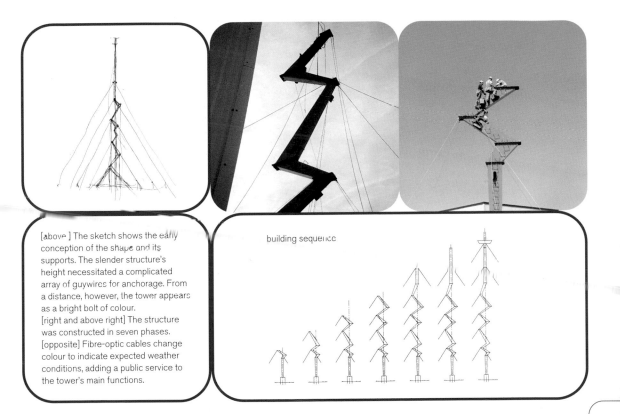

[above] The sketch shows the early conception of the shape and its supports. The slender structure's height necessitated a complicated array of guywires for anchorage. From a distance, however, the tower appears as a bright bolt of colour.
[right and above right] The structure was constructed in seven phases.
[opposite] Fibre-optic cables change colour to indicate expected weather conditions, adding a public service to the tower's main functions.

building sequence

Birkerts's cellular tower marks the interchange of two expressways near the town, but it also marks a change in the landscape and airspace, heralding the future of wireless telephone communication and acting as a messenger for the natural and man-made worlds.

building bridges

Bridge-Master's House
Purmerend, The Netherlands
UN Studio

Increasingly, when civic architecture produces something of aesthetic quality the general population has a feeling of getting lucky, as if infrastructure and thoughtful design were at opposing ends of the bureaucratic development spectrum. The architects of UN Studio see it differently and have set out on a deliberate path to unite architects and engineers in municipal planning. Convinced that the two professions 'have to learn to work together in a new, non-hierarchical relationship', they also find that questions need to be addressed about 'how to optimize this connection' and how to effect 'control and motivation in a new and better way of organizing utilitarian structures'.

The Bascule Bridges project in Purmerend demonstrates that this idea is more than pie-in-the-sky utopian manifesto. The bridge is formed by three decks that open and close in graceful succession to allow for passing watercraft. But the design excels in an array of public functions, such as linking a new housing development to the main road and providing pedestrian and cycle routes and one lane for cars. The structure also allows for a cycle path below and extra boat moorings along the river.

The bridge-master's house is a small, slightly skewed rectangular block whose slender profile refrains from impeding views along the bridge or waterfront. Inside, the bridge's elements are controlled with information gathered by technical facilities at ground level and communicated upstairs for the bridge-master; his quarters include domestic spaces and workrooms. To increase the transparency of the bridge house, perforated steel plates were applied around the concrete core, a solution that makes the interior of the house's lower half partly visible and emphasizes the architects' aim of a clear and fully integrated vision of form and function.

upper-level plan

ground-level plan

[above] Perforated steel plates and a slender profile running along the waterway ensure that the bridge-master's house embodies transparency rather than obstruction.
[left] The house combines domestic space with workrooms that receive information from technical equipment at ground level.

By harmonizing the formal qualities of the structure with innovative engineering, the architects achieved a sleek statement of functional purity.

bared minimum

Water Tower
Miyagi Prefecture, Japan
Atelier Hitoshi Abe

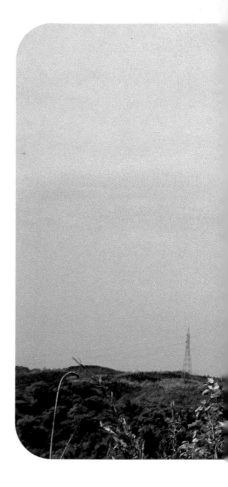

That a structure is meant to hold 136 tonnes of water at a height of 27 metres necessarily implies the desire for a substantial bulwark. Yet Hitoshi Abe's solution, graceful spiralling strands of stainless-steel mesh wrapping functional equipment in a webbed cone, creates a remarkably low-impact projection from the surrounding undeveloped landscape. Set on a base of reinforced concrete, the three-storey steel frame provides all of the vertical and horizontal stability needed of a water tower, while adhering to the rather contrary requisite that it blend with the natural setting. To achieve these two distinct aims, Abe first established the physical necessity of the vertical rectangle and then 'recomposed' the shape by breaking it down along the lines of force, softening the overall outline to a more sympathetic silhouette.

Hitoshi Abe is known for eschewing solid block forms for lighter, more intricate assemblages. This paring down of the functional to allow a building to be subsumed into its surroundings is something that he approaches with unique interest and finesse. The water tower's form is 'a kind of structural strip-tease', Abe says. To ensure that the building is fully assimilated into the landscape of dense foliage, ivy will be encouraged to grow over the stainless-steel skin, becoming, in Abe's words, 'an

architectural negligee'. Bedroom metaphors aside, the
Miyagi tower certainly opens up the definition of the water
tower, or at least encircles it with greater, though perhaps
more subtle, expectations.

'The uniformity of the tower is weakened as much as possible while maintaining its structural capacities'

[this page] The three-storey tower must hold 136 tonnes of water, so the vertical stability needed reinforcing through a sufficiently wide horizontal base. Sections reveals that the cone is actually slightly asymmetrical.
[above, right and opposite] The tower's structural latticework reduces its visual impact and will eventually become overgrown with vines to further blend the structure with the natural environment.

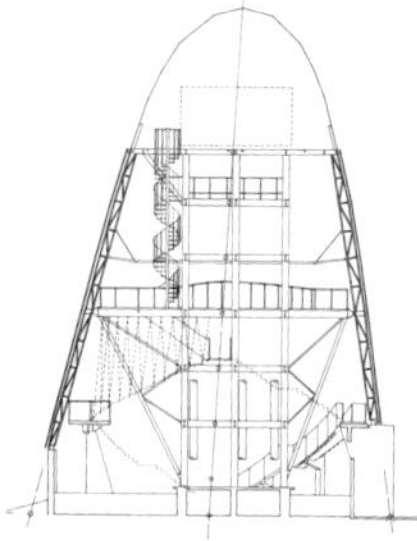

section

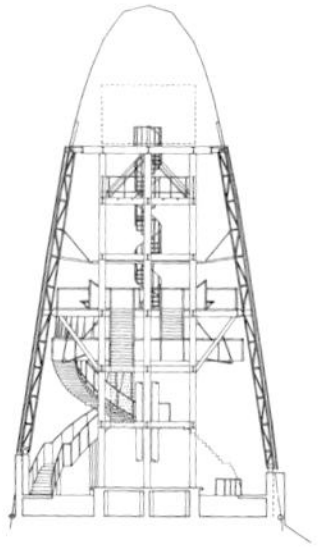

section

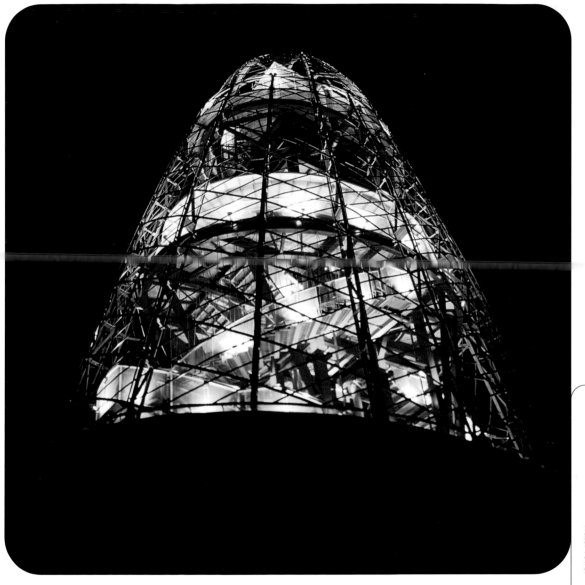

weathering heights

Thames Water Tower
London, England
Brookes Stacey Randall

Surges in the water supply have never been celebrated so well or so beautifully as in Brookes Stacey Randall's Thames Water Tower in west London. It is one of the city's three vertical tower pipes that accommodate surges in the water supply, which occur due to climatic pressure changes. The idea of making the function visible, on display as a public barometer, was proposed by Damien O'Sullivan and Tania Doufa, then students at the Royal College of Art, London.

Brookes Stacey Randall designed a 16-metre tower that is divided into five sections, each with its own arrangement of water nozzles that are linked electronically to a barometer switching device. The barometer detects pressure changes and then controls the level from which the water is sprayed onto the glass. It then sets off sprays of specially treated and blue-dyed water at different levels within the tower according to the pressure. The entire mechanism is solar-powered, with energy provided by photovoltaic panels mounted on the top of the tower.

Considered a 'model of responsive building', the tower is located in a busy roundabout, part of a new, 130-kilometre London ring road, and appears to stand in salute to that engineering achievement. Observers see a structure that increases in sophistication as it grows in height. At ground level, the plant and pump machinery is encased in matt-finished stainless-steel plate. Rising above, the surge pipe itself is clad in a mirror-finished stainless-steel sheeting that is visible through the toughened glass cylinder. Visibility, in fact, became the point of the exercise, as the architects ensured that surfaces and details were polished to reflective brilliance and chose black silicone sealant for its graphic effect. The information-age Trajan's column is topped by a solar vane and lightning mast, functional elements that subtly crown a structure that is both intelligent building and art.

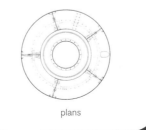

plans

[previous pages and opposite] The architects' aim was visibility, which they achieved by using mirror-finished stainless steel to clad the surge pipe within a wholly transparent cylinder of toughened glass.
[left] The 16-metre-tall tower is divided into five sections, and each has its own arrangement of water nozzles that spray organically dyed water onto the inner face of the glass cylinder in response to water pressure.

The most visible of London's three pipes that allow for surges in the water supply, the tower is a statement of architectural and atmospheric intensity.

shedding light

Garden Shed and Workshop
Oslo, Norway
Carl-Viggo Hølmebakk

When is a garden shed not a collapsing timber hut partly covered in overgrowth? When it's a three-storey cylindrical tower designed by Carl-Viggo Hølmebakk for his parents' house in Oslo. Though a tower 6.5 metres tall might not seem the most obvious choice for a utility room, this structure's vertical form derives not from whimsy but from genuine practical considerations: a lack of space in a densely wooded site and a desire to keep the many mature pine trees in the garden landscape, as well as a need for storage space and a workshop.

Hølmebakk's design occupies a modest footprint (under 4 metres in diameter) and consists of a single layer of half-brick laid in stretcher bond and capped with an arcing fibreglass roof. The brick-and-timber dialogue is continued with doors of horizontal pine boards that form an interlocking pattern with the toothed-brick doorframe (achieved by leaving alternating courses of brick to protrude along each side). By not cutting a doorway and by attaching an inner structure comprising a galvanized-steel staircase, timber shelving and benches to the timber roof supports – 'like a tea strainer in a teacup' – rather than the walls, Hølmebakk preserved an elegantly uninterrupted brick skin, a perfect cylindrical tribute to bricks and mortar.

Housing a workshop on the middle level with storage space above and below, the circular tower is perhaps reminiscent of medieval fortified structures or Romanesque towers, but the interior is bathed in natural light, not at all the dark and foreboding place suggested by those historic forms. Indeed the general impression is one of lightness, not only because of the roof's translucence but because of its 'floating' quality, making this garden monolith something of a gentle giant among common sheds.

[right] The three-storey stair and shelving structure is independent of the brick skin, supported instead by the roof frame. Through the transparent roof, natural light suffuses the space. [opposite] The toothed-brick doorframe creates a woven effect with the vertical pine slats of the doors that continue the lines of the brick courses.

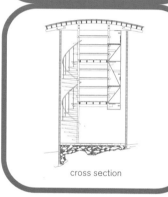

cross section

The architect preserved an uninterrupted brick skin, a perfect cylindrical tribute to bricks and mortar.

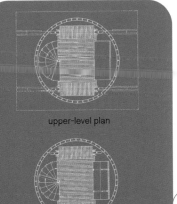

upper-level plan

middle-level plan

ground-level plan

anytime, anywhere

Collapsible, portable, made-to-order structures for a population in motion

Inasmuch as the end of the century has been about movement and speed in lifestyle, communication, distribution it has also been about human mobility and adaptability. We no longer live in the villages our parents did, or in the same kinds of structures. A house no longer means four walls and a roof or even a permanent structure. Container cabins, tree houses, a new spin on the old caravan idea – these are what the architects concerned with mobility envision as comfortable and suitable habitats for a population in motion for a few hours, a day or a lifetime. But these are not just playful attempts at putting a box on wheels; they are studied representations of an evolving philosophy of the essential transience of the human condition.

Lightweight and movable, these structures can be adapted not only to different purposes but to different, highly unusual sites. Designs that question traditional ideas of shelter, space and permanence all contribute something to the debate on what kinds of buildings the architecture of the future will produce. Decades ago film-makers and fiction writers envisioned that the landscape of the new millennium would be dominated by spacecraft and a decimated natural terrain. These mobile structures combine the advantages of space-age materials and machine-cut modular fittings with a sensitivity to building in an environment that has shown remarkable endurance but is under threat. As a consequence of such thinking, most of these projects are easy to assemble, the more complex becoming self-contained, energy-efficient units.

Richard Horden's 'Ski Haus' and 'Silva Spider' represent our determination to inhabit the inhospitable and yet, having learned the lessons of our past determination to invade the natural world, to leave little trace of our invasion. His 'Fisch Haus' is also a gentle intrusion in the landscape, whether attached to the top of the car during transport or set on slender supports for a short stay. All three of these structures signify holistic thinking: the total weight, number of parts and assembly comply with the demand for easy construction and dismantling.

With all of these designs, it is the structure that does the adapting rather than the site. Instead of gouging out a wider road from a dirt track, the only access to the location of his High Sierra cabins, Wes Jones made sure the shipping containers he was using were utterly transportable and could be dropped in by helicopter. The containers themselves show an emphasis not only on the transportable but on the ideal of re-use.

Oskar Leo and Johannes Kaufmann's designs for the expandable 'Su-Si and Fred' are similar to shipping containers in shape but also in adaptability, allowing for simple expansion or addition without the need for extensive construction so that space can be achieved in a matter of hours but without sacrificing style.

Gilles Ebersolt has diverged from the box completely in his geodesic adaptations for work and play but he has also made an effort towards achieving non-permanent support by 'borrowing' the framework of giant trees for his 'Icos' treetop observation unit. Intended for less serious pursuits, his inflatable, rolling 'Ballule' could have serious influence on protective shelter. Similarly, Dominik Baumüller's rotating airborne shelter is a fascinating novelty and a significant departure from ground-built forms. Martin Ruiz de Azúa, in fact, produces a shelter that fits in a pocket, is self-inflating, and can be used on almost any site.

While many of the architects here pursue what we might call 'anti-permanence', the creators of 'Maison Valise' present the ultimate statement in portable, adaptable accommodation: an expandable suitcase habitation that highlights an emphasis on design over site, on multiplicity of functions over permanence. Parisian architects Claire Petetin and Philippe Grégoire see the old architectural monoliths of the traditional city not as obsolete but as a fitting backdrop for new, more nomadic units that are more suited to our fast-changing lifestyles. Their work goes beyond addressing human transience to embrace it as a natural and more environmentally friendly coexistence.

treehouse

'Icos' Treetop Observation Structure
Portable
Gilles Ebersolt

If only those eco-warriors, installing themselves in the branches of trees in an effort to save forest giants from the axe, had known about Icos. Designed by Paris architect Gilles Ebersolt to facilitate the observation and study of the forest canopy, Icos is a twenty-sided, aluminium-framed structure that is dropped into place using a specially equipped airship, and fixed with cables.

Assembly, which begins on the ground and is finished in situ, takes two people about two days. Thirty Dural rods are tied at twelve connection points to produce a geometric shape in a setting that suggests Buckminster Fuller meets Tarzan, but it is a marriage that is strangely well-matched. The inherent strength of the geometry is enhanced by the massive living bulwark of the trees.

Once Icos has been firmly tethered, modular furniture is hoisted up by rope and attached to the bearing structure. Then the interior space, which is no mere tent in the trees, can truly be appreciated. Four triangles, which form the base of the structure, have a floor made of multi-ply with one opening allowing access for visitors ascending by rope. Once inside, the inhabitants enjoy distinct spaces dedicated to the functions of work (observation), cooking and even a toilet facility. The cooking area has a surface for food preparation and storage pouches. The work terrace at the top is reached via an internal ladder. There, three swivel chairs, a safety rail and a mount for optical apparatus make the job of recording the natural habitat at dizzying heights seem almost comfortable. At the end of a day or night of

observation, the scientist or nature-lover can retire to one of three hammocks protected by a waterproof canopy and mosquito nets tucked neatly away in pouches.

    Not content to offer just a sturdy, effective shelter at such a leafy altitude, Ebersolt also equipped the structure with power achieved through the use of photovoltaic cells, and the capacity for storage of 100 litres of water. At a weight of between 50 and 100 kilograms, Icos is a model of energy and spatial efficiency, something no self-respecting eco-tourist or -warrior should do without.

[left and opposite] The structure is brought to the site by airship, having been partially built on the ground. Assembly continues once the structure has been firmly anchored to the branches of the host tree.
[below] The sketch shows the twenty sections created using thirty lightweight Dural bars arranged in equilateral triangles with twelve joints. With all of the fittings in place, the assembled unit weighs only 50 to 100 kilograms.

squaring off

'Su-Si' and 'Fred' Transportable Buildings
Made to Order
Kaufmann 96 Architektur

They sound like a couple you might invite to dinner, and indeed you might. Oskar Leo and Johannes Kaufmann have come up with a response to demands for instant space: 'Su-Si and Fred', two transportable buildings for use as a single-person dwelling, studio, office space or home addition. The design offers the ultimate in flexible working and living and makes relocation or expansion 'as quick and uncomplicated as possible'.

The units are transported by truck and erected on site using a mobile crane. Production takes five weeks, but installation of your new office-extension-microhabitat takes a mere five hours for the 30- to 50- square-metre

Su-Si model or a downright speedy two hours for all 18 square metres of Fred, much less time than it would take to repaint the dining room, much less add on an extension.

It's not quite flat-pack architecture, but almost. The frameless structures conform to road transport standards and have the built-in bonus of modern, sophisticated design. The smaller version expands from 9 to 18 square metres using electronically controlled sliding wall elements. Both versions feature kitchen, bath and sleeping area, and Su-Si can be placed on space-saving stilts so that a car can be parked underneath. The pair are

made using wood construction with glazed wall and window openings.

And yet, the prefabricated, modular approach does not preclude individual expression. Whereas Fred can be expanded or contracted on site, Su-Si is available in different sizes. The customer can select different woods or other materials, as well as the interior finishes. Variations include the ever-popular blond wood with metal accents and a womblike dark-red veneer. With flexibility and efficiency like this, Su-Si and Fred stand out in a crowd, not as hasty add-ons, but as good, truly adaptable design.

[right] The plan and section show the range of functions, from standard living facilities to under-floor car-parking that Su-Si has to offer. Though not expandable, Su-Si comes in different sizes: length from 10 to 14 metres and width from 3 to 3.5 metres.
[below] Both models conform to road transport standards.
[opposite, below right and far right] A finished Su-Si model with spruce floor, glazed sections and red-veneered interior.

Su-Si: plan

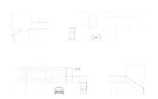

Su-Si: elevations

[left] The Fred unit is put into place with the help of a mobile crane. Once on site Fred can be fully assembled in two hours.
[below] The plan shows the expanded and minimal configuration of Fred, while the interior view shows the structure on stilts.
[opposite] Fred expands from 9 to 18 square metres and, like Su-Si, is available in a variety of materials. The furnished structure is an inspired home or office.

Fred: interior view

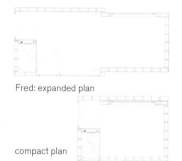

Fred: expanded plan

compact plan

climbanger...
Ski Haus, alpine shelter
Portable
Richard Horden

Alpine conditions do not immediately suggest lightweight design. However, English architect Richard Horden and his team of students in Munich approach their micro-architecture with 'a fascination for the beauty of nature, and the elegance and lightness with which aeroplanes and yachts move through the air, wind and water'. This attention to aesthetic quality and mobility has resulted in a number of portable structures that are as beautiful and light as they sound, structures that make a virtue of delicate contact with the site in accordance with the diktat to 'touch the earth lightly'.

The idea for the ski haus was conceived while the architect was out skiing late high in the Alps and wondering if it would be possible to stay for any length of time in that setting comfortably. This 'mobile alpine hut' or 'hard tent' was developed after a series of sketches, weight calculations and meetings with helicopter pilots. If the shape of the ski haus is familiar, it is probably because it was modelled on the principles of helicopter design, making transportation by air fast and efficient.

Like many of his 'microtecture' projects, it is also designed to stand without foundations, using its own

built-in support structure, so that it will 'leave no trace' once it has been dismantled. Horden believes in learning from all forms of building and encouraging students to be conscious of the entire process of design, from sketches to models to the impact and weight of the finished volume in its context. The fact that many of his students have produced structures that can be transported in minimal packaging and assembled on site (see pages 46–49, 186–91) is a tribute to the completeness of his design vision and the artful fusion of technologies.

[previous pages and left] Ski haus's shape was inspired by helicopter design to minimize the 'down-wash' effect from the helicopter rotors during transport.

[opposite below] With its self-securing structure, the ski haus requires no foundations.

[below] The shape deflects falling snow and prevents it from gathering around the base, leaving a hollow beneath that allows access in deep-snow conditions.

front elevation

plans

Horden believes strongly in forming relationships with and adapting from industry, particularly vehicle manufacture. Such 'technology transfer' helps him and his students to advance their 'lightweight building concepts for future-oriented forms of construction'.

[above] Once it has been dropped onto place and secured, the ski haus's solar roof panels provide energy for the cabin. It is designed to accommodate two people.
[right] Inspired by a wish to spend a significant amount of time in fairly inhospitable conditions, the Ski Haus may not blend with the surrounding landscape but as a temporary, autonomous, self-supporting unit, it will leave no more than a footprint behind.

outer sphere

'La Ballule' Inflatable Sphere
Portable
Gilles Ebersolt

Paris architect Gilles Ebersolt specializes in the lightweight, the inflatable and the all-terrain structure, but his ideas of mobility differ from recent developments in transportable modular units that can be carried to and assembled in urban sites or countryside. Ebersolt's 'La Ballule' is not just mobile in the sense of being easily assembled, however, it actually moves. The inflated 4-metre sphere, with an inner sphere of 2 metres, is made to roll down mountainsides, sand-dunes or ski slopes. Ebersolt himself descended Mount Fuji while safely cushioned inside La Ballule and has survived drops of up to 10 metres.

Made of polyurethane, the skin is extremely elastic and can resist tearing from sharp rocks and other hazards. Numerous black indentations that make La Ballule look like a giant golf ball are actually points of connection between the inner and outer sphere. Once the object has been inflated using a small generator pump,

the inner sphere is accessed through a small tunnel.

Although the inflatable sphere has been down waterfalls, Ebersolt does not recommend a trip down Niagara Falls. 'You have to be very careful because the Ballule could go very fast,' he warns. To be perfectly protected, he advises filling it with Helium gas, to give it more lift, or increasing the size of the exterior sphere for extra padding in particularly steep or rough terrains.

Though the Ballule offers a small amount of insulation from cold, it is primarily designed 'for play' and can only accommodate one person at a time. Given the amount of injuries sustained from extreme downhill sports, it is a wonder we have not yet seen the safe Ballules springing up (or down) the slopes of Europe. This very adult version of the bouncy castle seems just the thing for the intrepid, should they find themselves at the top of a seductive incline or just feeling the need for a little added protection.

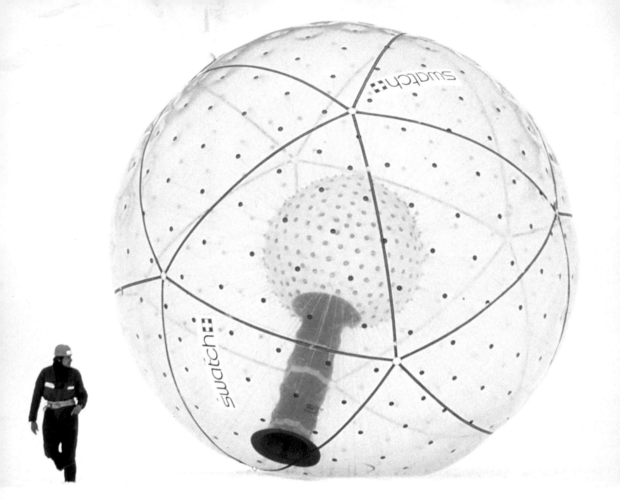

Though it has the appearance of a small golf ball inside a larger transparent golf ball, La Ballule is actually an air-filled polyurethane sphere capable of sustaining drops of more than 10 metres with a person cushioned safely inside.

Like many of Gilles Ebersolt's creations, La Ballule reflects a fascination with geometry and inflatable structures. While the object is intended mainly for fun, the elasticity of its skin and air cushion reflect serious developments in all-terrain protection.

acts of containment

Mountain Cabins
California, USA
Jones, Partners: Architecture

Re-use and adaptability have become watchwords of twenty first-century architecture. From loft apartments to warehouse galleries to power-station art museums, functional structures are being recast to serve new uses. In the most successful of these recycling programmes, the new function is enhanced by the building's original purpose-built features. Such is the case with the modified 6-metre shipping containers that Wes Jones has commandeered to serve as guest cabins. They were originally designed for two professors at Stanford University who wanted to build guest quarters and outbuildings for students and staff on a 360-acre site among forest and meadows in the High Sierra mountain range. Since they would only be used during brief periods, the quarters needed to demonstrate extreme durability with respect to security, weather conditions and fire. Given the portable nature of Jones's design, it's clear that the container mountain cabins can be used for just about any site.

Being hardy, inexpensive and, as the architect points out, 'eminently transportable', shipping containers have been used as temporary shelters around the world and offer a range of benefits; they are also well-suited to a modular approach. The low-cost containers allow room

in the budget for numerous modifications, while the standardized size means that the entire thing can be shop-fabricated, further reducing costs. The transportable nature of the containers was of utmost importance for the untamed terrain. The only access is by a narrow dirt track, so the units themselves are delivered by helicopter. Once in situ, the 'telescoping design' fits together rather like an exploded axonometric – literally exploding the box. Yet even with so much functionality popping out at all angles, the most extraordinary design feature is its unchallenging attitude to the beauty of the rugged natural surroundings.

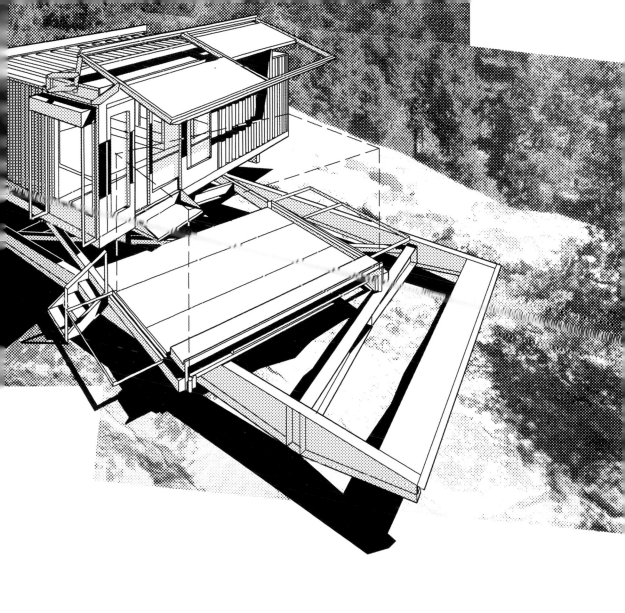

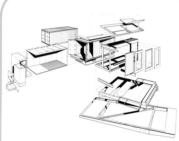

exploded axonometrics/
assembly sequence

[above] The containers can be
delivered to the site by helicopter, thus
avoiding the necessity of gouging out
access routes.
[left] The 'telescoping design' and
shop-fabricated elements produce
a neat, modular, inexpensive, site-
assembled unit that assumes a variety
of forms and functions.
[opposite] Once unpacked, the
exploded container seems right at
home in the rugged terrain.

plan

front elevation

side elevation

In addition to the flexibility of features built into the containers, the structures have been carefully articulated as modules to produce in one instance a circular colonylike arrangement and in another a vertical stack that becomes a library tower.

In the quest for reductivist design, temporary shelters offer a fruitful area of experiment. Richard Horden delights in portable, holistic design, and the seasonal or site-specific structure is a logical expression of that aim, especially when it endeavours to fold itself up and leave any setting virtually untouched.

The Fisch Haus and Silva Spider may differ in their inspiration, but as takeaway shelters they are in close company. The former was derived from traditional huts used by fishermen along the Danube. Instead of modifying the familiar wooden box on stilts, however, Horden and his students moulded aluminium and carbon fibre to form a 'habitable car-top cabin', or 'cuddle cabin'. Once the structure's folding leg supports have been deployed, the car can be driven away. While atop the car, the 45-kilogram cabin can be accessed through the car-roof window and uses energy from the car's power system. At the end of a stay, Fisch Haus's legs are retracted for the journey to the next location.

The unfolded, freestanding Fisch Haus resembles its design cousin in form as in principle, consisting of a roughly triangular volume supported by three aluminium legs. When designing the Silva Spider, Horden explains, they looked at spiders and asked 'Why eight legs', with the answer having something to do with a variation in functions that a portable shelter need not achieve.

Nevertheless, with three fully movable aluminium legs, the Silva Spider does emulate the insect model in its manipulation of compression and tension and in its employment of the principle of tensegrity. This remarkably adaptable framework can 'accommodate itself to any topography and will find a firm footing even in gorges and in gaps between buildings'. The plastic cabin is glass-fibre reinforced, with an aluminium honeycomb core and acrylic glass window elements. Side flaps can be raised like sun canopies, and there is room enough inside for two: Spiderman, perhaps, and his more comfort-minded accomplice.

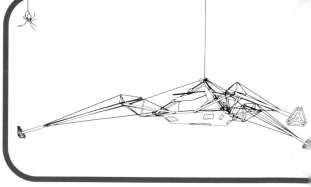

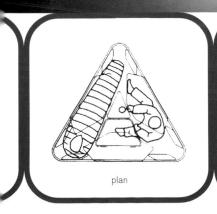

plan

section

[left] Inspired by the arachnid's adaptability, the Silva Spider has three fully movable aluminium legs, which, using the compression principles of tensegrity, enable it to find a footing in the most difficult sites, including rocky gorges or gaps between buildings. [above] The cabin accommodates two people. A photovoltaic coating on the exterior provides energy for a battery that powers the structure's heating and lighting.

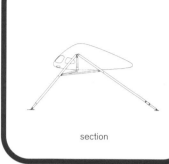

section

The Fisch Haus has come a long way from the elevated Austrian huts on the Danube that inspired it. Similar to the Silva Spider, it consists of a two-person cabin perched on slender aluminium supports.

The 45-kilogram car-top cabin can be accessed through the roof of the car. Once a site has been chosen, the legs unfold to produce a free-standing structure. Power is obtained through the use of solar panels and from the car's battery.

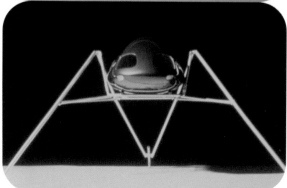

While Horden is eager to explore new technologies, his micro-architecture projects reflect a desire to achieve 'a direct experience with nature' while leaving the natural setting untouched.

Imagine a giant, flexible, hovering Frisbee. Now imagine sipping wine under its protective canopy in a light rain. This is the 'rotating pneumatic umbrella', the creation of Dominik Baumüller, who developed the idea of using centrifugal force to stretch a membrane in space.

The mushroom-shaped 'Rotation Pneu' can actually achieve various forms depending on the speed of rotation and wind forces. Made up of a double membrane, the 'pneu' is inflated using a cavity between the layers that receives ambient air through inlets positioned near the axis. Under rotation, air flows into the cavity and the centrifugal force inflates the membrane. The uninflated shape is that of a toroid, which gives the appearance of a ghostly floating presence, though it is anchored with supports at the top. A small, 300-watt motor attached to a plywood centre causes the device to rotate. As it does so and the force of the air entering the membrane increases, the fabric spreads until it reaches its full extent as a spinning, disc-shaped umbrella that can be used for temporary shelter or as a marquee, or lit from within for art installations or even used as a projection screen.

Weighing about 18 kilograms, Baumüller's prototype has a 6-metre diameter and is made of polythene fleece. He claims that inflation is simpler than with a single-membrane umbrella because the air entering the membrane only has to be accelerated with the help of the motor to make it expand. Since the 'Pneu' is sensitive to high wind speeds, you might in stormy weather have to find somewhere else to sip your wine and watch the spectre of the 'pneu' hovering freeform in the distance.

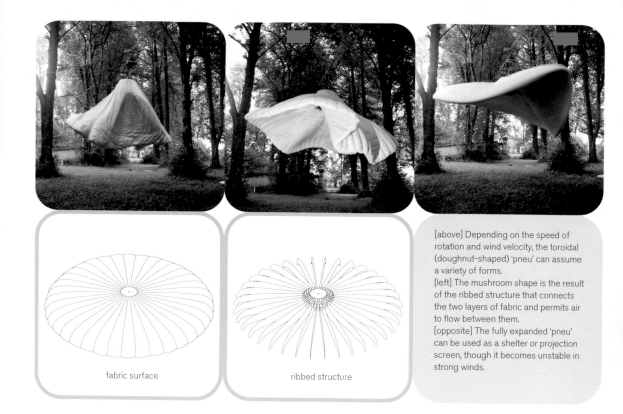

fabric surface

ribbed structure

[above] Depending on the speed of rotation and wind velocity, the toroidal (doughnut-shaped) 'pneu' can assume a variety of forms.
[left] The mushroom shape is the result of the ribbed structure that connects the two layers of fabric and permits air to flow between them.
[opposite] The fully expanded 'pneu' can be used as a shelter or projection screen, though it becomes unstable in strong winds.

Following early attempts by such innovators as Frei Otto to use rotational forces to unfold an umbrella without the use of solid elements, Baumüller has created a seemingly free-floating, somewhat ethereal, pneumatic structure.

water spirit

Floating Pavilion
Groningen, The Netherlands
Maki and Associates

The Dutch have long been known for their affinity with water and all things maritime. In the spirit of this tradition, Japanese architect Fumihiko Maki designed a floating pavilion, a concrete barge with a spiralling canopy that can be used to host a wide range of live performances, from concerts and plays to poetry readings.

The key words that inspired his creation, which was executed in collaboration with the city of Groningen and Antwerp-based producer Dora van Groen, were 'silence, space, movement, play, dream, water, change and freedom'. Made of white translucent polyester canvas stretched over 'a double-helical web of light steel tubes and cables', the delicate canopy is attached to a 150-square-metre barge that also houses dressing rooms, bathrooms and storage for performers in its 2.8-metre

depth. The audience can be seated on the barge itself on perforated steel benches, or those same benches can be tipped to make the entire ship a theatrical backdrop.

As it wends its way through the countryside the billowing silhouette has the quality of a spirit rising from the mists. Cast against the green of the forest, it reminds the architect of a 'white swan'. Illuminated for evening performances, its form assumes the less elevated appearance of a nocturnal snail. Maki seems less concerned with such earthly comparisons than with the changing 'reciprocal relationships created among environment, citizens and architecture' as the pavilion adapts to location, function and audience. Versatility being an admirable trait of any performer, viewers are bound to be lost in awe of such a dynamic achievement.

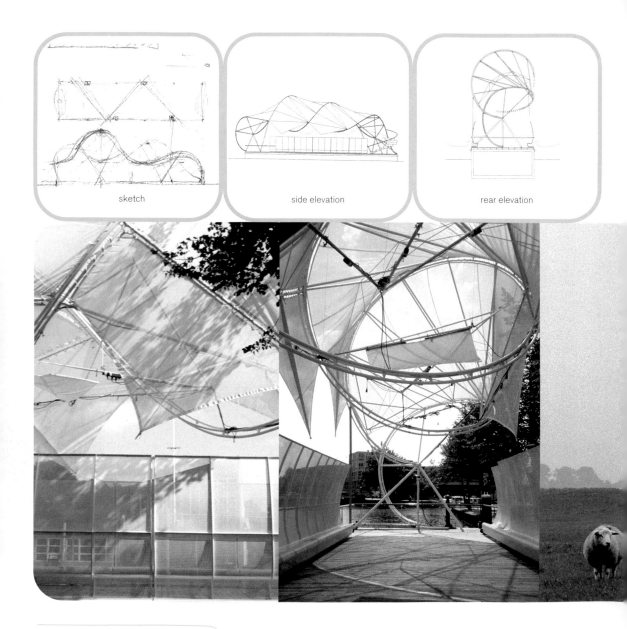

sketch

side elevation

rear elevation

anytime, anywhere

[opposite] Drawings reveal the spiralling double-helical form of the framing beneath the canopy.
[below] The multifunctional pavilion's ethereal quality is enhanced by the billowing canvas canopy, a seemingly inflated form that is actually anchored to an inner structure of lightweight steel tubes precisely tensioned with steel cables. Thus, a 25-metre concrete barge has the appearance of weightlessness.

'The pavilion's spirit was developed using a poetic matrix of keywords: silence, space, movement, play, dream, water, change and freedom.'

grandes idées
'Maison-Valise' Housing Unit
Portable
TimeZone

Paris architects Claire Petetin and Philippe Grégoire, of the studio TimeZone, live and design by the maxim that less is more. For them, however, it is not a statement of the sublime beauty of minimalism but of the ability to change the face of the rigid urban landscape through the development of small, temporary structures that are by definition, compact, utilitarian and non-monumental. Their 'maison-valise' emerged from a desire to resolve the difference between the city's static architectural fabric and the essentially transient nature of the human population and experience.

In reaction against futile attempts to match the needs of an ever-changing populace with an existing urban fabric or creating still more immovable structures, Petetin and Grégoire created a mobile unit that adapts to individual or family requirements. Because they are unanchored structures, the total number in any given context could change according to the needs of a city.

The model was exhibited in Berlin, a city of frenzied building but also home to the nomadic groups that partly inspired the architects to construct their expandable mobile units. But their aim is not just to house the homeless. Spurred by the notion of 'abandoning the strict separation of the domestic space of the home and the public space of the street', the architects hope to see maison-valises springing up in the developed commercial zones rather than confined to their own caravan park

on the city's periphery. This would force the interaction between two sides of an unreconciled urban conflict (the physical and the temporal).

In other words, this flexible unit might change our perception of and in the cityscape. As the team experiments with lightweight, durable construction materials, such as those used for sports equipment, they may yet find a way to achieve their grand design.

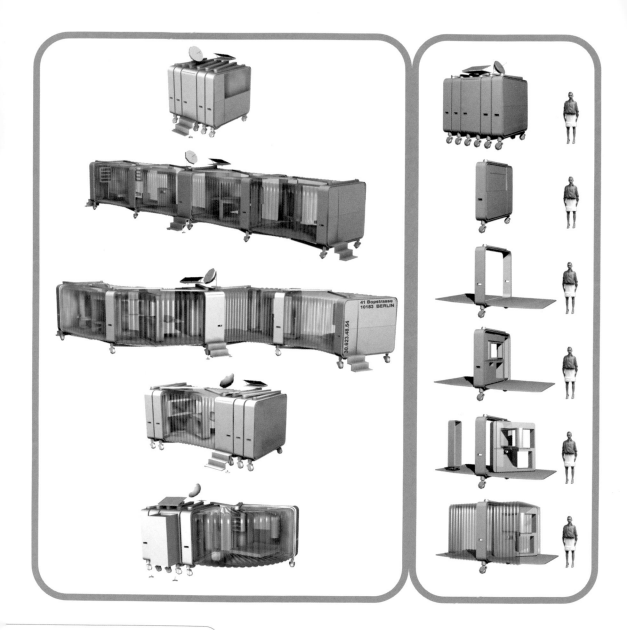

On the unit is printed:

41 Bopstrasse
10183 BERLIN

30.623.48.54

[above] Petetin and Grégoire have developed the maison-valise as a mobile, flexible housing unit that can expand or contract in size and number according to the needs of the population. The existing urban architecture would serve as a fixed backdrop for the continually changing arrangement of units.

[left] To achieve their design, the architects are experimenting with lightweight, durable materials and configurations.

The architects do not simply propose a new kind of temporary housing for the homeless or a mobile-home park: they want to change the face of the city itself.

Maison-Valise

It is a house so basic it only has one room, so easy to use it requires no assembly and so portable it fits in your pocket. Martin Ruiz de Azúa set out to design a dwelling that defied the modern demand for products that satisfy our every desire and addressed instead the basic need for shelter. 'Cultures that maintain a more direct relationship with their environment show us that the habitat can be understood in a more essential and reasonable manner,' he argues. If his inflatable house does not convince people to pare down their living requirements, it at least reminds us that life need not be as complicated as we sometimes believe.

Ruiz's description of the Basic House comes across like a manifesto: 'I propose an almost immaterial house that expands when triggered by body or solar heat. A house so versatile that, by turning it onto one side or the other, it protects from cold or heat, so light that it floats and, moreover, that can be folded and stored in a pocket.' In short, 'having it all while hardly having anything.'

What the basic house does have is an interior area of 8 cubic metres made from double-sided metallic polyester. The reversible fabric is gold on one side to protect against cold, and silver on the other to insulate against heat. Once you have made your choice of interior-exterior climate colour, the tidy bundle, which weighs in at 200 grams when deflated, can be inflated simply by allowing air into the fabric.

As air enters the circular aperture in the 'floor', the house inflates and the inhabitant can enjoy a fully enclosed environment, which, thanks to the translucent material, is bright and allows for pleasantly filtered panoramic views. The feeling is of being inside a tent, but without any cumbersome framing elements. The essential difference comes at sunset, as the 'house' gradually deflates to become an enveloping blanket, which you can inflate the next day or pocket and move on.

[above] Assembly is effortless: simply allow air through the hole at the bottom of the fabric and a new house is born. Inside, the fabric allows filtered views to the outside.
[left] Double-sided metallic polyester provides protection against heat and insulation for the cold — and it makes an appealing landmark in any context.

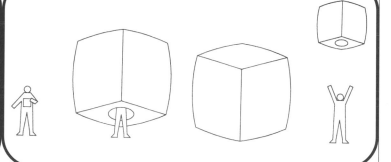

sources

Project Credits • Architect Information
Index • Picture Credits

project credits

Kielder Belvedere (pp 020–023)
Client: The Kielder Partnership
Cost: £40,000
Size: 4.9 m (length, sides) 1.4 m (radius of interior circular shelter)
Architects: Softroom (Chris Bagot, Josephine Pletts, Oliver Salway, Dan Evans)
Structural engineer: Brian Eckersley. Contrctor: Forum Ltd. Groundworks: Ian Reeve. Stainless steel cladding to front elevation: Avesta Sheffield. Acid-etched cladding, textured stainless-steel cladding to door and galvanized steel roof sheathing: Rimex Metals Ltd. Coloured glass skylight: Global Glass Technology Ltd. Seat: Durcon Fabrications Ltd. Roof membrane: Lastite.

'Shroud for Bathing' (pp 024–027)
Client: Jacqueline Vance
Cost: $60,000
Size: 37.2 m² (total area)
Architects: Eskew+, New Orleans: R. Allen Eskew (principal); Steve Dumez (design director); B.J. Siegel (project architect); Nick Marshall, Jose Alvarez, Vincent Bandy, Marianne Makdisi, Matthew Kymes (project team)
Consultant: Ove Arup & Partners (membrane)

Tea Houses (pp 028–031)
Client: Made to order
Cost: DM 30,000
Size: 5.76 m² (each)
Designer: Shigeru Uchida
Manufacturer/designer's representative: Studio 38, Wawerla

Sauna Pavilion (pp 032–037)
Size: 37 m² (total area)
Architect: Artifact Design + Construction: Christopher Kilbridge, Salvatore Tranchina (partners-in-charge)
General contractor: Quadresign; custom door fabricator: Zachary-Siff Group

Palm Beach Studio (pp 038–041)
Size: 12.8 m² each (bedroom and studio)
Architects: dawsonBrown Architecture: Robert Brown, Jeff Karskens, Sharon Fraser (project team)
Builder: Manuel Talbot (Northern Design and Building); copper roof: Juerg Wilk (Architectural Roofing and Wall Cladding)
Structural engineer: John Ryder (Ove Arup and Partners).

'GucklHupf' (pp 042–045)
Client: Wörndl, Automaten Comp.
Size: 24 m²
Architect: Hans Peter Wörndl
Production team: Claudia Dias, Christian Eppensteiner, Michael Karassowitsch, Antje Lehn, Richard Mlynek, Elisabeth Semmler

Point Lookout (pp 046–049)
Exhibit: Mount Lofty Architectural Conference
Size: variable
Architect: Richard Horden. Australian crew: Scott Read, Russell Jones, Bill Cuneo, Andy Edwards, Chris Exner, Sarah McCarthy
Design team: Sarah Forbes Waller, Richard Horden, Russel Jones, Sarah Kirby
Construction: Formula Spars, Lymington

Park Lodges (pp 054–057)
Client: The Hoge Veluwe National Park Foundation
Size: 30 m² (each)
Competition design: MVRDV – Winy Maas, Jacob van Rijs and Nathalie de Vries, with Elaine Didyk
Design: MVRDV – Winy Maas, Jacob van Rijs and

Nathalie de Vries with Joost Glissenaar, Elaine Didyk, Jaap van Dijk
Structure: ABT, Velp. Building physics: DGMR, Arnhem.
Contractor: Wolfswinkel bv, Hoenderloo

Community Mailbox Enclosure (pp 058–061)
Client: Cranbrook Community
Size: 21 m², 3.7m (height)
Architect: Dan Hoffman; assistance: Patricia Royer, Sandra Wheeler, Jason Vollen

Copenhagen Architecture Park (pp 062–065)
Organizer: Kirsten Kiser
Size: 65 m² (each)
Architects: Mario Botta, Michael Graves, Ralph Erskine, Heikkinen-Komonen, Arata Isozaki, Josef Paul Kleihues, Leon Krier, Henning Larsen, Richard Meier, Enric Miralles, Dominique Perrault, Richard Rogers, Aldo Rossi

School Bus Stop (pp 066–069)
Client: Schoolchildren of Nearing Road
Cost: $1,400
Size: 3.3 m²
Architects: Michael Culpepper, Greg Tew

Nature Overlook (pp 070–075)
Client: Maryhill Museum of Art
Cost: $100,000
Size: 112 m²
Architects: Allied Works/Brad Cloepfil
(principal/designer), Corey Martin
(project lead)
Engineer: Ang Engineering Group
General contractor: Hard Rock Concrete

Storytelling Pavilion (pp 076–079)
Client: Cranbrook Academy
Size: 10.4m², 3.7m (height)
Architect: Dan Hoffman. Assisting: Mark
Kolodziejczak, Jason Vollen, Alfred Zollinger

'Black Maria' and 'Gisant/Transi' (pp 080–085)
Exhibit: Sezon Museum of Modern Art, Karuizawa
Size: 19.5 m² ('Black Maria'); 27 m² ('Gisant/Transi')
Architect: Hiroshi Nakao; associate: Hiroko Serizawa
Contractor: Manzzo Koumusho

'Hairy House' (pp 086–089)
Client. English Heritage
Cost: £10,000
Size: 9 m²
Designer: Thomas Heatherwick

Gateway Structure (pp 094–097)
Client: City of Miami Beach
Architects: Wood and Zapata: Carlos Zapata,
Benjamin Wood (principals in charge);
Anthony Montalto, Rolando Mendoza,
Fred Botelho (design team)
Engineers: William Faschan, Leslie E. Robertson
Associates (structural)
General contractor: S.I. Nicholas

Train Station and Bicycle Shed (pp 098–101)
Client: Keifuku Railway Co., Ltd.
Size: 365 m²
Architects: Shuhei Endo Architect Institute:
Shuhei Endo (architect); Aoi Fujioka
(project staff)
Structural engineer: Shinichi Kiyosada
Construction: Nakamitsu Kenzai Co., Ltd

project credits

211

Electricity Masts (pp 102–05)
Client: Gemeente Rotterdam
Cost: NLG 600,000 (market square, details and circular road)
Size: 3.1 m (height)
Architects: West 8 Landscape Architects & Uban Planners: Adriaan Geuze, Erik Overdiep, Dirry de Bruin, Leon Emmen

Public Lavatories and Flower Kiosk (pp 106–09)
Client: The Royal Borough of Kensington and Chelsea
Cost: £190,000
Size: 60 m²
Architects: CZWG Architects; executive project architects: Stansfeld & Son
Structural engineer: Dewhurst Macfarlane and Partners.
Quantity surveyor: Orbell Associates
Main contractor: R. Mansell Limited; brick manufacturers: Shaws of Darwen; brickworkers: M. Gibbons; structural steelwork: Metals Galore Limited; glazing: Alan Hone Limited; aluminium clock and cast aluminium and timber benches: IF

Newspaper Kiosk (pp 110–13)
Client: Ali Hussein
Cost: DM 100,000
Size: 5 m²
Architect: Jörg Joppien Architekten

Metro Stops (pp 114–19)
Client: ÜSTRA Hannoversche Verkehrsbetriebe AG
Cost: DM 16.9 million
Architects: Despang Architekten – Günther Despang, Martin Despang, Marc Wiese, Nicola Uthe, Martina Ludewigs
Project management: TransTeC-bau; construction engineering: Ove Arup and Partners; special construction engineering: Bergmann + Partner; lighting: Fahlke + Dettmer

Modular Shelters (pp 120–23)
Client: Stanford University
Cost: $6,000 per bay
Size: 9 to 112 m²
Architects: Jones, Partners: Architecture – Wes Jones, Doug Jackson, Michael Gough, Bernard Chang, Bob Shepherd, Jim Rhee

Bus Shelter (pp 124–27)

Client: JC Decaux Deutschland
Size: 5.1 m (length)
Architects: Eisenman Architects, New York City: Peter
Eisenman (principal); Richard Rosson (associate architect);
Sergio Bregante (project architect); Peter Lopez, Sven
Pfeiffer (project assistants)
Engineer/Consultant/General contractor: JC Decaux

Park Lavatories (pp 132–35)

Client: Hyogo Prefecture
Size: 119 m² (building); 54 m² (floor area)
Architects: Shuhei Endo Architect Institute
Structural engineer: TIS & Partners.
Construction: Nakamitsu Kenzai Co., Ltd

Cellular Telephone Relay Tower (pp 136–39)

Client: Airtouch Cellular Inc.
Size: 15.3 m (height)
Architects: Gunnar Birkerts
Counsel: DiClemente Siegel Design Inc.
Engineers: Malouf Engineering, Engineered Endevors Inc.,
Landmark Tower Corp.
Construction: Rudolph/Libbe

Bridge-Master's House (pp 140–43)

Client: City of Purmerend
Cost: NGL 141,100,000
Size: 12 m (height of bridge-master's house); 36 m²
(ground floor area)
Architects: Ben van Berkel (UN Studio/Van Berkel &
Bos); project team – Freek Loos (coordination), Ger Gijzen
Consultants: Ingenieursbureau, Amsterdam

Water Tower (pp 144–47)

Client: Miyagi Prefecture
Size: 270 m² (area); 27.6 m (height)
Architects: Atelier Hitoshi Abe; co-architects: Shoichi
Hariu Architect and Associates
Structural engineers: S.D.G. Mechanical engineers: Sogo
Setsubi Keikaku; contractors: Miyagi Komuten

Thames Water Tower (pp 148–53)

Client: Thames Water Utilities Ltd.
Size: 16 m (height)
Architects: Brookes Stacey Randall – Andrew Fursdon,
Paul Voysey, Simon Innes, Nik Randall, Michael Stacey.
Concept: Damian O'Sullivan, Tania Doufa
Engineer: Atelier One. Contractor: J Murphy and Sons Ltd

Garden Shed and Workshop (pp 154–57)
Client: G. and I-S. Hølmebakk
Size: 65.5 m (height); 4 m(diameter)
Architect: Carl-Viggo Hølmebakk

'Icos' Observation Structure (pp 162–65)
Client: made to order
Cost: estimate on request
Size: 3.2 m (diameter)
Weight: 100 kg (including fittings)
Architect: Gilles Ebersolt
Manufacture: Gilles Ebersolt with Claude Leblois
Technical School

Su-Si and Fred (pp 166–71)
Client: made to order
Cost: Su-Si: 1,000,000 ATS excl. VAT
Fred: 600,000 ATS excl. VAT
Size: Su-Si: 30–50 ; Fred: 9–18 m²
Weight: Su-Si: 8–12 tons; Fred: 4 tons
Architects: Oskar Leo and Johannes Kaufmann

'Ski Haus' [prototype] (pp 172–77)
Size: 13.5 m²; 2.4 m (height)

Architect: Richard Horden; design team: Ken Boyd,
Richard Horden, Sarah Kirby, Benjamin Knight; test crew
design team: Marco Bomio (mountain guide); Daniel
Brunner (helicopter pilot)
Construction: Barient Sparcraft and Amalgam

'La Ballule' (pp178–81)
Client: made to order
Cost: FFr 68,000
Size: 4 m (exterior diameter); 2 m (interior diameter)
Architect: Gilles Ebersolt
Manufacture: PTS France

Mountain Cabins (pp 182–85)
Client: Lambertus Hesselink and Denise Kroll
Cost: $350,000
Size: 27–149 m²
Architects: Jones, Partners: Architecture – Wes Jones,
Doug Jackson, Michael Gough, Bernard Chang, Bob
Shepherd, Jim Rhee

'Silva Spider' [prototype] (pp 186–89)
Size: 5.3 m²; 1.4 m (height)
Weight: 130 kg

Architects: Richard Horden; Jürgen Amann and Thomas Wenig (students); Andreas Vogler (coaching)
Consultant: Tim Brengelmann, Professor R Barthel

'Fisch Haus' [prototype] (pp 190–91)
Weight: 45 kg
Architects: Richard Horden; Gerhard Abel, Ursula Hammerschick, Silvia Hörndl, Martin Janecek, Birgitta Kunsch, Paul Linsbauer, Christopher Lottersberger, Michael Quixtner, Magrit Rammer, Hannes Schillinger, Sakura Watanabe (students); Helmut Richter (chair); Willi Frötscher, Anne Wagner, Andreas Vogler (coaching)

'Rotation Pneu' (pp 192–95)
Client: Made to order
Size: 6 m diameter (fully inflated)
Weight: 18 kg
Architect: Dominik Baumüller

Floating Pavilion (pp 196–99)
Client: City of Groningen, The Netherlands
Size: 150 m² (floor area)
Architects: Maki and Associates; collaborator: Dora van Groen

Contractors: Wilma Bouw (concrete), Volker Stevin Materieel (steel), Merinens Groningen (tent), Henderico (carpentry), Bolt (rigging)

Maison-valise (pp 200-03)
Client: Made to order
Cost: c. 450,000 francs
Size: 1.9 m²; 2.2 m (height)
Architects: TimeZone: Claire Petetin, Philippe Grégoire

'Basic House' (pp 204–07)
Client: Made to order
Cost: c. $50 (estimated)
Size: 8 m³ (inflated)
Weight: 200 g (deflated)
Designer: Martin Ruiz de Azúa
Fabric manufacture/development: Paï Thio

architect information

Atelier Hitoshi Abe
30–30 Takimichi, Aoba-ku
Sendai, Miyagi
981 Japan
tel: +81 (0)22 278 8854
fax:+81 (0)22 277 7933

Allied Works Architecture Inc.
2768 NW Thurman
Portland, Oregon 97210
USA
tel: +1 503 227 1737
fax: +1 503 227 6509

Artifact Design + Construction
121 W. 27th Street, Suite 705
New York, NY 10001
USA
tel: +1 212 206 7945
fax: +1 212 206 7946
artifactonline.com

Dr Dominik Baumüller
Pappenheimstrasse 7 Rückg.
80335 Munich
Germany
tel/fax: +49 (0)89 555 411
dominikbaumueller@sulloon.de

Gunnar Birkerts Architects Inc.
1830 E. Tahquamenon
Bloomfield Hills, Michigan 48302
USA
tel: +1 248 626 5661
fax: +1 248 626 5101
www.gunnarbirkerts.com

Brookes Stacey Randall
Architects & Technology Consultants
New Hibernia House
Winchester Walk
London SE1 9AG
UK
tel: +44 (0)20 7403 0707
fax: +44 (0)20 7403 0880
info@bsr-architects.com

Michael Culpepper
1220 Boren Avenue, Suite 708
Seattle, Washington 98121
USA
tel: +1 206 521 3509
fax: +1 206 012 7868
mculpepper@zgf.com

CZWG Architects
17 Bowling Green Lane
London EC1R OOB
UK
tel: +44 (0)20 7253 2523
fax: +44 (0)20 7250 0594
mail@czwgarchitects.co.uk

DawsonBrown Architecture
Level 1
63 William Street
East Sydney
NSW 2010
Australia
tel: +61 2 9360 7977
fax: +61 2 9360 2123

Despang Architekten
Am Graswege 5
30169 Hanover
Germany
tel +49 (0)511 88 28 40
fax: +49 (0)511 88 79 85
Despang @BauNetz.de
www.DespangArchitekten.de

Gilles Ebersolt
60, rue Truffaut
75017 Paris
France
tel: +33 (0) 1 42 29 39 74
fax: +33 (0) 1 42 29 86 69
gilles.ebersolt@wanadoo.fr

Eisenman Architects
41 W. 25th Street, Floor 11
New York, New York 10010
USA
tel: +1 212 645 1400
fax: +1 212 645 0726
earch@idt.net

Shuhei Endo Architect Institute
Soan., 1-7-13, Edobori, Nishi-ku
Osaka 550-0002
Japan
tel: +81 6 6445 6455
fax: +81 6 6445 6456
endo@tk.airnet.ne.jp

Eskew+
Architecture Environments Urban Design
1 Canal Place
365 Canal Street, Suite 3150
New Orleans, Louisiana 70130
USA
tel: +1 504 561 8686
fax: +1 504 522 2253

architect information

Thomas Heatherwick Studio
16 Acton Street
London WC1X 9NG
tel: +44 (0)20 7833 8800
fax: +44 (0)20 7833 8400
mail@thomasheatherwickstudio.co.uk

Dan Hoffman
Arizona State University
School of Architecture and Environmental Design
P.O. Box 871605
Tempe, Arizona 85287-1605
USA
tel: +1 480 965 8757
fax: +1 480 965 0968
dan.hoffman@asu.edu

Carl-Viggo Hølmebakk
Sofiesgate 70
0168 Oslo
Norway
tel/fax: +47 22 46 76 00

Richard Horden
Horden Cherry Lee Architects Ltd
34 Bruton Place
London W1J 6NR
UK
tel: 44 (0)20 7495 4119
fax: 44 (0)20 7493 7162
hcla@hcla.co.uk

Jones, Partners: Architecture
141 Nevada Street
El Segundo, California 90245
USA
tel: +1 310 414 0761
fax: +1 310 414 0765
bossarch@well.com

Jörg Joppien Architekten
Köpenicker Strasse 48/49
10179 Berlin
Germany
tel: +49 (0)30 204 50 690
fax: +49 (0)30 204 50 692
jjoppien@compuserve.com

Kaufmann 96 Architektur
Sägerstrasse 4
6850 Dornbirn
Austria
tel: +43 (0) 5572 26283
fax: +43 (0) 5572 26283-4
office@kaufmannkaufmann.com

Kirsten Kiser (Copenhagen Architecture Park)
kirstenkiser@arcspace.com

Maki and Associates Architecture and Planning
13-4 Hachiyama-cho Shibuya-ku
Tokyo 150-0035
Japan
tel: +81 3 3780 3880
fax: +81 3 3780 3881

MVRDV
Postbus 6316
3002 JC Rotterdam
The Netherlands
tel. +31 10 4772860
fax: +31 10 477 3627
mvrdv@archined.nl

Hiroshi Nakao
Nakao Serizawa Architects
Ginrei-Hall 602, 2-19
Shinjuku
Tokyo 162-0825
Japan
tel/fax+ 81 3 3235 2902
nasa@gw4.gateway.ne.jp

Martin Ruiz de Azúa
Valencia 179 50 1a
08011 Barcelona
Spain
tel/fax +34 9 3453 8827
mrazua@teleline.es

Softroom
34 Lexington Street
London W1F OLH
UK
tel. +44 (0)20 7437 1550
fax: +44 (0)20 7437 1566
softroom@softroom.com

Greg Tew
School of Architecture
160 Cheever Hall
Montana State University
Bozeman, Montana 59717
USA
tel: +1 406 586 1846
gtew@montana.edu

TimeZone
Claire Petetin Philippe Grégoire Architectes
142 rue de Faubourg Saint-Denis
11010 Paris
France
tel: +33 (0)1 40 37 20 37
fax: +33(0)1 46 07 68 95
petetin-gregoire@compuserve.com

UN Studio
van Berkel & Bos
Stadhouderskade 113
1073 AX Amsterdam
The Netherlands
tel. +31 (0)20 570 2040
fax: 31 (0)20 570 2041
info@unstudio.com
www.unstudio.com

Shigeru Uchida
Studio 80
1-17-14 Minami-Aoyama
Minato-ku
Tokyo 107
Japan
tel: +81 3 3479 5071
fax: +81 3 3475 4586

Studio 38, Wawerla
Eichhofstrasse 38
24116 Kiel
Germany
tel: +49 (0) 431 544 88 618
fax: +49 (0) 431 544 88 619

West 8 Landscape Architects and Urban Planners
P.O. Box 24326
3007 DH Rotterdam
The Netherlands
tel: +31 (0)10 485 58 01
fax: +31 (0)10 485 63 23
west8@west8.nl

Hans Peter Wörndl Architekt
Dornbacherstrasse 107
A-1170 Vienna
Austria
tel/fax: +43 1 486 1102
woerndl@magnet.at

Wood and Zapata
100 South Street
Boston, Massachusetts 02111
USA
tel: +1 617 728 3636
fax: +1 617 728 3635
mkoff@wood-zapata.com

index

Atelier Hitoshi Abe 144–47
Allied Works Architects 70–75
Architecture Park 62–65
Artifact Design + Construction 32–37
'La Ballule' Inflatable Sphere 178–80
'Basic House' 204–7
Dominik Baumüller 192–95
Gunnar Birkerts Architects 136–39
'Black Maria' 80–85
Mario Botta 62–65
Bridge and Bridge-master's House 140–43
Brookes Stacey Randall 148–53
Bus Shelter 124–27
Cellular Telephone Relay Tower 136–9
Community Mailbox Enclosure 58–61
Michael Culpepper 66–69
CZWG 106–9
DawsonBrown Architecture 38–41
Despang Architekten 114–19
Gilles Ebersolt 162–5, 178–81
Eisenman Architects 124–7
Electricity Masts 102–5
Shuhei Endo Architect Institute 98–101, 132–35
Ralph Erskine 62–65

Eskew + 24–27
'Fisch Haus' 186–91
Floating Pavilion 196–99
Garden Shed and Workshop 154–57
'Gisant/Transi' 80–85
Philippe Grégoire 200–3
GucklHupf 42–45
'Hairy House' 86–89
Thomas Heatherwick Studio 86–89
Heikkinen-Komonen 62–65
Dan Hoffman 58–61, 76–79
Carl-Viggo Hølmebakk 154–57
Richard Horden 46–49, 172–77, 186–91
'Icos' 162–65
Jones, Partners: Architecture 120–23, 182–85
Jörg Joppien 110–13
Kaufmann 96 Architektur 166–71
Kielder Belvedere 20–23
Kirsten Kiser 62–65
'Maison-Valise' 200–3
Maki and Associates 196–99
Maryhill Nature Overlook 70–75
Metro Stops 114–19
Miami Gateway Structure 94–97

Modular Shelters 120–23
Mountain Cabins 182–85
MVRDV 54–57
Hiroshi Nakao 80–5
Newspaper Kiosk 110–13
Palm Beach Studio 38–41
Park Lavatories 132–35
Park Lodges 54–57
Dominique Perrault 62–65
Claire Petetin 200–3
'Point Lookout' 46–49
Public Lavatory and Flower Kiosk 106–9
'Rotation Pneu' 192–95
Martin Ruiz de Azúa 204–7
Sauna Pavilion 32–37
School Bus Stop 66–69
'Shroud for Bathing' 24–27
'Silva Spider' 186–91
'Ski Haus' 172–77
Softroom 20–23
Storytelling Pavilion 76–79
'Su-Si and Fred' Transportable Buildings 166–71
Tea Houses 28–31
Greg Tew 66–9

Thames Water Tower 148–53
TimeZone 200–3
Train Station and Bicycle Shed 98–101
UN Studio, van Berkel & Bos 140–43
Shigeru Uchida 28–31
Water Tower 144–47
Wood and Zapata 94–97
Hans Peter Wörndl 42–45

picture credits

4 (top to bottom): Keith Paisley, Neil Alexander, Nacása & Partners Inc., David M Joseph, Robert Brown, Paul Ott, Richard Horden, Christian Richters, Chistina Capetillo; 5 (top to bottom): Christian Richters, Michael Culpepper/Greg Tew, Sally Schoolmaster, Balthazar Korab, Nacása & Partners Inc., Keith Paisley, Wood and Zapata, Toshiharu Kitajima, Jereon Musch, Chris Gascoigne; 6 (top to bottom): Markus Becket, Despang Architekten, Jones, Partners: Architecture, Christian Richters, Yoshiharu Matsumura, Balthazar Korab, Christian Richters, Atelier Hitoshi Abe, Peter Durant, Jiri Havran; 7 (top to bottom): L. Pyot/OCV-PN/Eurelios, Ignacio Martínez, Alex Kallenberger/Richard Horden, Gilles Ebersolt, Jones, Partners: Architecture, Richard Horden, Tobias Lehn, Berthold & Linkersdorff, TimeZone, Daniel Riera.

9 (left to right): Keith Paisley, Neil Alexander; 10–11 (left to right): Nacása & Partners Inc., David M Joseph, Robert Brown, Paul Ott, Richard Horden, Christian Richters, Christina Capetillo, Christian Richters, Michael Culpepper/Greg Tew, Sally Schoolmaster; 12–13 (left to right): Balthazar Korab, Nacása & Partners Inc., Keith Paisley, Laura Paresky, Toshiharu Kitajima, Jereon Musch, Chris Gascoigne, Markus Becket, Despang Architekten, Jones, Partners: Architecture, Christian Richters; 13–14 (left to right): Yoshiharu Matsumura, Balthazar Korab, Christian Richters, Atelier Hitoshi Abe, Peter Durant, Carl-Viggo Hølmebakk, L. Pyot/OCV-PN/Eurelios, Ignacio Martínez, Alex Kallenberger/Richard Horden, Gilles Ebersolt, Jones, Partners: Architecture, Richard Horden, Tobias Lehn, Kei Mizui, Daniel Riera.

20–3: Keith Paisley; 25–7: Neil Alexander; 29–31 Nacása & Partners Inc.; 33–7: David M Joseph; 39–41: Robert Brown; 42–5: Paul Ott; 47–9: Richard Horden; 55–7: Christian Richters; 59: Balthazar Korab; 60–1: Christina Capetillo; 63–5: Christian Richters;

67–9: Michael Culpepper/Greg Tew; 70–5: Sally Schoolmaster; 77–9: Balthazar Korab; 80–5: Nacása & Partners Inc.; 86–7: Kieran Gaffney/Thomas Heatherwick Studio; 88: Thomas Heatherwick Studio; 89: Keith Paisley, 91–7: Laura Paresky; 98–101: Toshiharu Kitajima; 103–05: Jereon Musch; 106–09: Chris Gascoigne; 111–13: Markus Becket; 114–19: Despang Architekten; 120–23: Jones, Partners: Architecture; 124–27: Christian Richters; 133–35: Yoshiharu Matsumura; 137–39: Balthazar Korab; 141–43: Christian Richters; 144–47: Atelier Hitoshi Abe; 148–53: Peter Durant; 155, 157 (bottom): Jiri Havran; 156, 157 (top): Carl-Viggo Hølmebakk; 162–65: L. Pyot/OCV-PN/Eurelios; 167–71: Ignacio Martínez; 173–77: Alex Kallenberger/Richard Horden; 179–81: Gilles Ebersolt; 182–85: Jones, Partners: Architecture; 186–91: Richard Horden; 193–95: Tobias Lehn; 197: Berthold & Linkersdorff; 198: Kei Mizui; 199: Berthold & Linkersdorff; 200–03: TimeZone; 205–07: Daniel Riera

209 (left to right, top to bottom): Keith Paisley, Neil Alexander, Nacása & Partners Inc., David M Joseph, Robert Brown; 210 (left to right, top to bottom): Paul Ott, Richard Horden, Christian Richters, Chistina Capetillo, Christian Richters, Michael Culpepper/Greg Tew; 211 (left to right, top to bottom): Sally Schoolmaster, Balthazar Korab, Nacása & Partners Inc., Keith Paisley, Wood and Zapata, Toshiharu Kitajima; 212 (left to right, top to bottom): Jereon Musch, Chris Gascoigne, Jones, Partners: Architecture, Markus Becket, Despang Architekten; 213 (left to right, top to bottom): Christian Richters, Yoshiharu Matsumura, Balthazar Korab, Christian Richters, Atelier Hitoshi Abe, Peter Durant; 214 (left to right, top to bottom): Jiri Havran, L. Pyot/OCV-PN/Eurelios, Ignacio Martínez, Alex Kallenberger/Richard Horden, Gilles Ebersolt, Jones, Partners: Architecture, Richard Horden; 215 (left to right, top to bottom): Richard Horden, Tobias Lehn, Berthold & Linkersdorff, TimeZone, Daniel Riera.

Gift of

The John W. Bowman Family

in memory of

TIMOTHY DILLON BOWMAN

First published in 1990 in the United States of America by
Rizzoli International Publications, Inc.
300 Park Avenue South, New York, New York 10010

Library of Congress Cataloging-in-Publication Data

Courtney-Clarke, Margaret, 1949–
    African canvas / by Margaret Courtney-Clarke ; foreword by Maya
Angelou.
        p.   cm.
    Includes bibliographical references.
    ISBN 0-8478-1166-2
    1. Art, Primitive—Africa, West—Pictorial works. 2. Art,
Black—Africa, West—Pictorial works. 3. Women artists—Africa,
West—Pictorial works. 4. Vernacular architecture—Africa, West—
Pictorial works.   I. Title.
N7398.C68   1990
709'.66—dc20   89-24037
                                                              CIP

Map by Lundquist Design, New York
Composition by David E. Seham, Associates
Printed and bound in Japan

Design by Massimo Vignelli

Page 1: Olife Agu adding the final touches to the family Obi, *a place of meeting. "I used to collect these colors near the water for my mother. It is our Igbo tradition but now people want American houses." Nokwa, Nigeria*

Pages 2-3: Olife draws the obo-aka, *"picture of the hand," while her daughters, Uduchukwa and Nneka, paint the carved wooden panel.*

Pages 4-5: Detail of the wooden door, akika, *carved by the late Edwin Agu in 1953 and painted each year by the women of the compound. Nokwa, Nigeria*

Pages 10-11: The obo-aka *pattern signifies a clean hand, a righteous person.*

Contents

ACKNOWLEDGMENTS *13*
FOREWORD *Maya Angelou* *16*
INTRODUCTION *19*
COMPOUND *25*
PAINTING *69*
MOTIFS *155*
INTERIORS *185*
BIBLIOGRAPHY *204*

In memory of my mother, Constance

This book would not have been possible without the support, love and rare understanding of my beloved companion, Cesare Bellici, who died unexpectedly after my final field trip. He traveled with me in spirit and in heart. He guided me, he nursed me through emotional turmoil and physical illness after each journey, and he gave me the courage each time to return to Africa. I have lost my friend and partner.

My father's interest and concern on this project has always been closely felt and appreciated despite the many miles which separate us. Both my parents played a vital role in teaching me about Africa and her way of life. Without their wisdom and inspiration, I doubt that I could have managed alone.

I gratefully am indebted to my friends and family around the world for their constant support and enthusiasm. In particular, I would like to thank Lauren Shakely for getting me started on this enormous task and for guiding it throughout with such warmth and sensitivity; Charles Mann who gave of his time and professional expertise to structure the outline and help with the development; Valerie Cann for her generous assistance and inestimable trust in many, many ways; David Goldblatt for his drive and persuasion all the times I wanted to give up in despair; and Massimo Vignelli who, once again through his insight into my work, has expanded the vision of an art through his design.

I am most grateful, too, to Maya Angelou for her extraordinary enthusiasm and contribution. Her understanding of women, of Africa, and of life's struggles will enrich future generations.

At Rizzoli, I would like to thank all those I have worked with over the past six years for making me feel at home. In particular, Gianfranco Monacelli for his unfailing reassurance and faith in my work and Solveig Williams for her personal involvement and dedication at all levels and throughout the development of this book.

All through my travels in West Africa, people provided warm hospitality, guidance and assistance:

In Nigeria: Chiobi Ekpechi, Dr. Alhassan Abudulai, Amos Obuamah, and Dr. Chike Aniakor;

In Ghana: Brothers Alhaji and Sulemana Abudulai, Alfred Salia, and James Adabugah and Salifu Abubakr from the Arts Council;

In Burkina Faso: Blanche Bationo, who also helped me in Mali, and the staff of the Centre National de la Recherche Scientifique et Technologique;

In Mali: the companies ODIK and Forafrique;

In Senegal: Patrick Dujarric, Tidiane Ngaido, Mauro Petroni and friends, and Italtekna;

In Mauritania: Mark Lynham, Mahfoudh ould Tah, and Sass ould Guig, mayor of Oualata.

I thank them all for their participation and for providing me with a basis for understanding their cultures.

A special thanks to my interpreters and drivers who not only assisted me through dozens of languages and countless dialects, but who also pushed vehicles through sand and dug them out of mud, who helped build roads, carried me through guinea-worm infested waters, and who helped me safely across tens of thousands of miles.

My greatest debt is to the women of rural West Africa who opened their homes to me, allowed me to enter their lives, fed me, nursed me through malaria, and shared with me a rich variety of their art. I collectively thank them for providing the focus of this book.

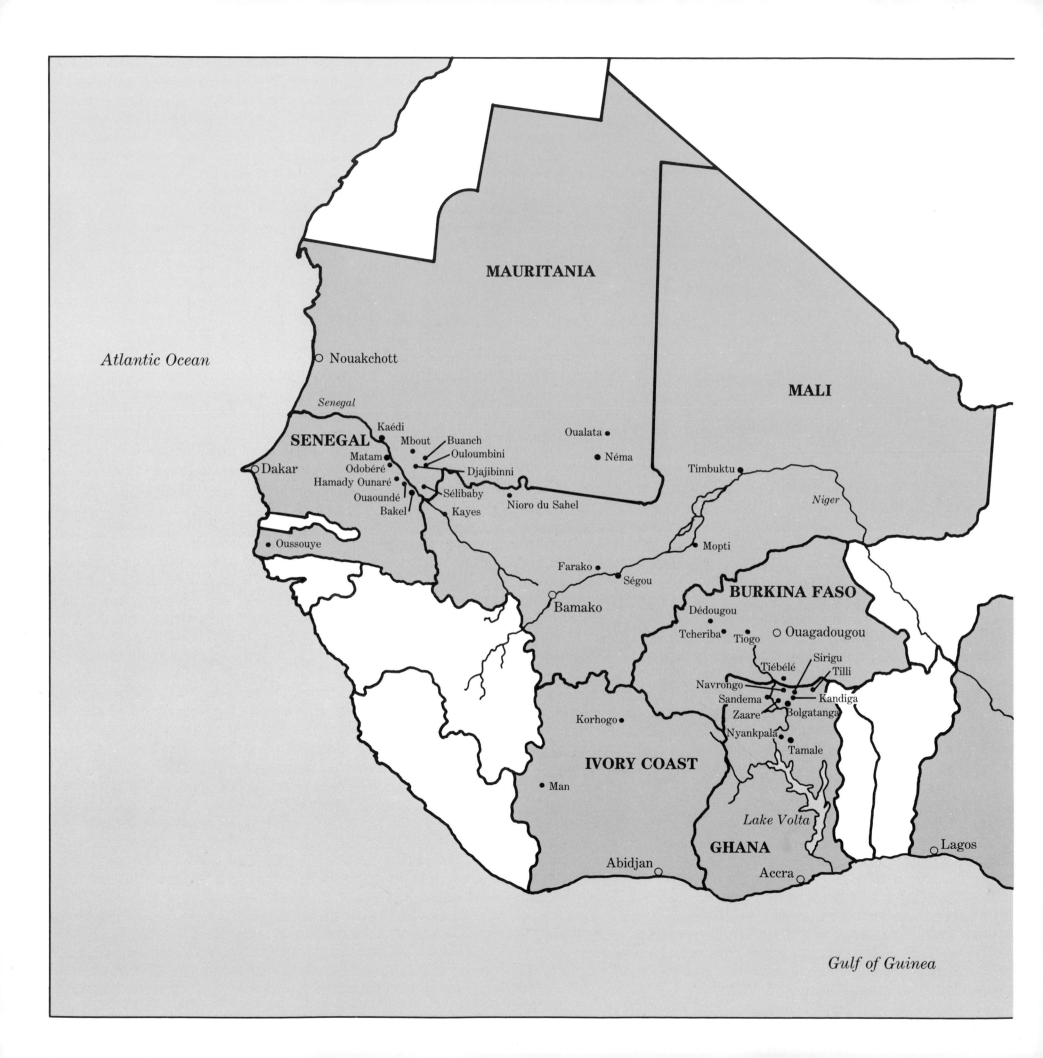

NIGERIA

Jos •

Abuja •

Yola •

Nsukka
•
Enugu
•
Awka
Onitsha •
•
Nri
Nokwa •
Abatete
Igbo-Ukwu
Nnobi

0   100   200   300   400   500   MILES

0   100 200 300 400 500 600 700   KILOMETERS

𝒩

Foreword

Heritage

What is Africa to me;
Copper sun or scarlet sea,
Jungle star or jungle track,
Strong bronzed men, or regal black
Women from whose loins I sprang
When the birds of Eden sang?
One three centuries removed
From the scenes his fathers loved,
Spicy grove, cinnamon tree,
What is Africa to me?
So lie, who all day long
Want no sound except the song
Sung by wild barbaric birds
Goading massive jungle herds,
Juggernauts of flesh that pass
Trampling tall defiant grass
Where young forest lovers lie,
Plighting troth beneath the sky.
                              Countee Cullen

Africa, as impression, as idea, lies deep in the labyrinth of human imagination. Often its shape is beyond the will of words and its silhouette below the strata of conscious recovery. It lives in all of us on a primordial level inexplicable but undeniable. We are the spring boughs with only the vaguest memory of winter's ruthless treatment of the tree. Despite a spate of nature documentaries, and despite endless shelves of travel books, Africa remains for most of us an ephemeral shadow, a hazy but personal observance.

True or contrived, or possibly true and contrived, African myths have wandered around the globe, half understood, half believed, half unbelievable, always adding to their mysteries and lack of comprehension. The unending human quest in Africa for treasure, that wild impulse toward the accumulation of precious metals, minerals, and even other human beings themselves, can account for some of the misconceptions of Africa and the erroneous fantastic descriptions of the place and its peoples.

No person with impunity could plough the earth for its bright gold and its glint of diamonds without determining that those wonderful elements were free booty only because they were found on "The Dark Continent."

The place of origin of Homo sapiens could not possibly be stripped of its strongest sons and daughters for greedy purposes unless one could name the place (and think of it) as not the "First," or even "Second," but the "Third World."

Thus, it would seem despite studies focused and degrees earned on the subject, that the land, its peoples, and its customs are unknowable. Nonetheless, books, speeches, essays, monographs, and folk tales inform us that human beings are more alike than we are unalike. Margaret Courtney-Clarke pleased the world with her photographic book called *Ndebele*, which captured the art of the women of southern Africa. She has brought the same direct eye and courageous spirit to look at the art and heart of West African women.

The successful movements and the unfortunate retreats of the human tribe are traceable through the folk tales, songs, detritus left by wars, and triumphal display of enemy totems captured after victories, and we may follow demographic shifts of families, clans, and tribes by assessing their search for food, water, safety, and arable land. We might conclude, then, that basic human need impels the species toward transition as well as preservation. But Margaret Courtney-Clarke's work leads us to another deduction: An irresistible need to define oneself and a curiosity about the intangible quality of nature might just as logically explain why groups of nomadic human beings elect to stay in semi-permanent homelands. Their art, the drawn descriptions of the known and unknown, might furnish the needed security in a world rife with insecurity. For millennia, men have described their masculine worlds, their worlds both tangible and spiritual. They have used wood, bronze, stone, and ivory. Their concepts of their universe gave shape to martial dances and substance to tales of battles of triumph and surrender. The un-named sun and uncounted stars were given character and place in their stories. The tides and seasons were recognized by the rhythms of the men's drums.

In Africa, as in other places of the world, women create their own portraits, distinctive portraits of themselves and their universe. They use cloth, beads, leather and clay to express their views of the real and abstract worlds. Beliefs, spirits, omens, djinns, disappointments, fears, and accomplishments are named, confessed, called, admitted, and explained in the women's designs.

Their art, like all art, means to delight the eye, console the troubled mind, appease the highest authority, and educate the children in the way of the world. The aim also, whether or not articulated, is to infuse and sustain the family in an appreciation for life and the expectation of beauty.

It is evident in this book that West African women, unlike their South African sisters, eschew the bright reds and other primary colors. They allow themselves the ocher, black, white, yellow and beige earth tones. They do employ blue, but it is the blue-black, electric indigo or the soft, subtle blue of West African mornings. The Yoruba, one of West Africa's most ancient and surviving cultures, has roots extending back to 300 B.C. They were and are an artistically advanced people whose symbols and mythologies are still in popular use and still influential after centuries. There is a Yoruba legend which explains the Creation of the Universe, Ife (the Yoruba Homeland), and Human Beings. The folk tale praises Olakun, the goddess of the seas, as being an expert weaver. She also is claimed to possess an outstanding talent in the dyeing of cloth. In an attempt to regain her power over the earth, taken away from her because she has acted rashly, Olakun challenges Olorun, the ruler of the sky, to a weaving contest. Olorun is aware of the power of the woman's art, and will not meet Olakun fairly. Rather, he sends a chameleon which is able to instantly imitate all the goddess's colors and patterns. She concludes that if a lowly chameleon, only in the service of Olorun, is able to hold his own against her talents, then assuredly

Olorun himself will defeat her. Thus, the woman's art of design and dyeing was never really matched or bested by man. She was merely taken in by man's trickery, and her balance of art was set askew because she lost her internal moral balance.

Among most West African societies, inner beauty is deduced to be the result of good moral character. The Yoruba love of moderation is expressed in their admiration of the cool character Iwu Tutu, which implies self-discipline, reflection and restraint. Beauty in the artefact is therefore the result of the union of moral excellence and physical skill. (Pat Oyelola, unpublished dissertation, Ibadan 1981.)

West African women's dress designs and patterns are said to set European standards for modern modes, and are often found transformed in Western magazines of high fashion. Most of the ancient designs, whether on cloth, walls of houses, or on earthenware, were inspired by proverbs and sayings. Today in some cases the meanings have been lost, but the illustrations have remained.

One popular West African design displays two and three rectangular forms criss-crossing on contrasting colored cloth. It is called *Lai Momo* which translates from the Ga as "Burnt Sticks." It comes from the saying "Wood once burned, and allowed to go out, will be more easily ignited than green wood, freshly hewn." When a woman attends a meeting of mediation wearing *Lai Momo*, she tells the gathering that she is more amenable to reconciliation than to continuing the strife. So, as in all African life, art functions, and function follows art.

Another proverb which provided inspiration for a Nigerian design found on adire cloth is "If you do not appreciate the things you have, other people will treat them with contempt." Great counsel for the young and good wisdom for the aged to agree upon.

Whether the arrangement of lines and colors have remembered roots in ancient maxims or not, there is a great aesthetic sensation which surrounds the crafts of painting, weaving, dyeing cloth and making pots. These women, using ordinary clay found in their river beds, and employing their hands as paint brushes, have developed a powerful invention for visual pleasure. Their crafts are also public statements of their personal creeds.

The simple materials are forged into plastic designs which will be as temporary as the length of time between rainfalls, and with no lasting staying power against the insistent sun. These artists, however, do not seem to need promises of longevity, nor do they exhibit a craving for notice out of the ordinary. In fact, one of the most notable characteristics of house painting

among West African women is the camaraderie found among the women sharing the creation of design. Family members and those attached by friendship often join together in the industry of decoration. When they do it is agreed that the principal owner will contribute the major design, but it is also expected that every woman will bring something of her own soul to add to the overall effect.

Courtney-Clarke traveled thousands of dusty miles to find these graceful women and their appealing art. I imagine that her own internal journey was far longer, and even more dramatic. She is a modern woman, a modern white woman, although admittedly a unique and courageous one. She must have been challenged to the end of her wits to make friends with women with whom she seemed to have so little in common. And be assured that friendships were made or these photographs would not be so immediate, and so accessible. If the viewer can learn a small degree of what Courtney-Clarke has seen and generously offers, then the art of West African house painting, pot making, cloth dyeing and body tattooing will be added to our composition of what we mean when we say "World Art."

"Art is the manifestation of the undying soul of the people. It is the aspect of their genius which is manifest in the great works, no less in the day to day utensils which they use, the cloth they wear and the ornaments with which they adorn themselves. In all these and more real artistic merit can be discovered and recognized." (Saburi O. Biobaku, Former Vice Chancellor of Lagos University, Nigeria.)

What is Africa to me? It is mysterious, it is exciting, and it has been made more wonderful and more knowable because of the women's art. The women of West Africa and Margaret Courtney-Clarke.

Maya Angelou
May 1989

Introduction

The art of Africa is a casualty of colonial exploitation, surviving principally in the museums of other countries.
—Nadine Gordimer

My objective in this book is to document an extraordinary art form—vernacular art and architecture in West Africa—that is not transportable and therefore not seen in museums around the world. It is an attempt to capture the unseen Africa, a glimpse into the homes and into the spirit of very proud and dignified peoples. In much the same way as I photographed the art of Ndebele women, I have drawn on my personal affinity for the art itself, for methods, design and form, rather than the socio-anthropological or political realities of a people or continent in dilemma. These images portray a unique tradition of Africa, a celebration of an indigenous rural culture in which the women are the artists and the home her canvas.

My love for Africa and her people is not rooted in any way to romance and adventure. I was born in Namibia, of Irish and English descent, and spent most of my childhood growing up on farms. The desert and veld were my playgrounds, the San, then called "Bushmen," and Nama my playmates. My grandfather, Francis Priestley Courtney-Clarke, was Secretary for South West Africa, then a mandated territory of the League of Nations, and later also Native Commissioner. His work among the ethnic people was of the highest commitment and dedication. My mother served as his secretary, and, as one of the few Europeans who spoke what was then an unwritten language—the language of the San—her life was equally intertwined with the life and culture of the people of Namibia.

From a very early age, I loved painting and drawing. Later, that interest developed into an awareness and concern for "Bushmen" painting and rock-engravings—about which I wrote several essays—and the architecture of Cape Dutch settlers, the subject of my first book. Though I left Africa twenty years ago to further my education in art and photography, my ties with her remain strongly rooted in what was a free and happy childhood.

As a photojournalist with a fundamental interest in art and design, I wanted to travel and record *that* particular aspect of African culture (observing and analyzing the socio-political problems and harsh realities of modern-day Africa is a task for specialists). My first project was the photography of colorful mural art of a southern African ethnic group living partly in South Africa and partly in their designated "homeland" of KwaNdebele.

Curious about a few pictures I had seen in books, I next began to research mural painting by women in West Africa. It soon became clear that because of the nature of this impermanent art form—mud walls, clay canvases, and indigenous pigments—not to speak of industrialization and modernization in a rapidly changing world, this art was vanishing at an alarming rate. The few articles and paragraphs in books that made reference to mural art either were outdated, sometimes by twenty years or more, or discussed it as simply a "backdrop" for anthropological or architectural studies. No one had seriously endeavored to bring to public attention the existence of a traditional rural life in Africa as expressed through women's art and its relationship to those who live in the dwellings. The numerous publications on African art deal primarily with masks and wood carving, bronzes and terra-cotta work, gold weights and jewelry, textiles and embroidery, tools and utensils—all made by men.

19

Wishing to make my own contribution to this neglected art by women, I set out for West Africa in 1986, convinced I would find what I was looking for, although I was not sure exactly where to look. My journey covered a period of three years and exacted such a toll on my health and personal life that I would never wish to repeat it; yet, I discovered more mural decoration—and even more enduring spirit among its makers—than I had expected. For primarily financial reasons, I chose to travel alone. This magnified the difficulties of the trip in many ways—not the least the sense of danger—but it was probably this very vulnerability as a woman alone that allowed me to enter the world of those I encountered.

In Africa, national borders define political, rather than geographic or ethnic boundaries—which Nigerian poet and Nobel Laureate Wole Soyinka condemns as "the artificiality, the arrogance, the exploitive motivations which went into the disposal of African peoples into nationalities." The Nankani and Kassena people of northern Ghana, for example, have descendants (some even immediate family) living across the border in Burkina Faso. The Lobi people live in a triangular region within the boundaries of Ghana, Burkina Faso and Ivory Coast; while the Toucouleur, by way of their semi-nomadic lifestyle, move back and forth between Senegal, Mauritania, and Mali.

Far from the capital cities of Accra, Lome, Lagos, and Dakar, and thus European influence and modernization, there are peoples who still live in the traditional way. Since all of the art I wanted to photograph was in these remote areas, accessibility was a constant and major problem. Roads are in poor condition all over West Africa, and bridges which were built during colonial eras have long been washed away. I could travel only during the dry season, which meant a few months shooting at a time. Even when conditions were good, driving meant trekking over sandy (or muddy) river beds or frequently stopping to gather stones and dead wood to rebuild sections of the so-called road. In Nigeria, the roads between major towns are fairly good, but armed marauders replace hardship with real danger. After a week in Lagos—a city rife with hustlers, thugs, slave traders, and black marketeers—I gladly accepted the advice of friends to fly to Enugu, the capital of Anambra State—and home of the Igbo people—in order to avoid driving through the rain forest regions where bandits strike night and day. Nonetheless, I was still stopped on two occasions by assailants who hurled strips of wood with four-inch protruding nails under the tires and dragged me and my driver from the vehicle—a common means of extorting money.

West Africa is hardly an inviting place for the visitor. The climate is intensely hot—the seasons are "wet" or "dry." The harmattan wind during the dry season blows fine red dust from the Sahara, reducing visibility to a couple of yards. Sanitation facilities are poor and in rural areas non-existent, while water is life-threateningly scarce. I vaguely recall a traveler's description I read some years ago about Africa offering enormous rewards for the singular visitor with time on his hands and a bent for traveling long distances! Nowhere is that truer than in West Africa. Distances between villages are not only great in themselves, but also intimidating because of the traveling conditions: heat, dust, and "roads" that are beyond description. Time seems to be of no consequence to West Africans. The Westerner must learn of its meaning on a continent where so much seems meaningless. In the course of my travels I often spent days in a village waiting for a vehicle—which might or might not have been available to hire—or three days on the side of a road in the hopes that a camel might pass or a donkey cart appear. (Of the ten months I spent in West Africa, I probably spent six months waiting!)

Transportation—or the lack thereof—was the most difficult logistical problem of my many journeys. The few countries that have car rental companies do not allow their vehicles out of the state capital nor hundreds of miles into the interior, let alone across borders. For the most part, I had to rely on local taxis, the *taxi brousse* (bush taxi), or "toto" buses as they are known in Ghana, and private cars rented to me by friends. Along the Senegal River, I used dugout canoes to reach villages on the Mauritanian side, often surreptitiously at night because I lacked the required re-entry visa which, in an irony that is typical of West African bureaucracy, is impossible to obtain. In Mali, I started out with a rented car which broke down on "the other side" of the Niger River. After waiting days for a ferry, I was able to continue my journey inland by hiring two mopeds: one for my two interpreters, another for myself and a guide. There were no roads to our destination. We returned to the banks of the Niger days later on one bike in one-hundred-fifteen-degree heat.

During my visit to Timbuktu, I became obsessed with the idea of journeying into the Sahara, to Oualata, where I'd heard that women have decorated their homes for centuries. In order to avoid some two thousand miles via Dakar and Nouakchott, I decided to head "straight" north from Bamako. Ten days later, on reaching Oualata I had lost count of my transport means: from military escort in jeeps to twelve-ton trucks (stopping every half hour to cool the engines) to camels to donkey carts. The wealth of material I was able to record, however, made the effort worthwhile.

For weeks on end I ate only goat meat and drank camel's milk and contaminated water. On other occasions, I ate dog, bush rat, insects, and foods I could not identify, and sometimes—for days—nothing at all. Throughout this experience, I was beset by the health difficulties that befall any Western visitor in Africa's interior. Cholera had broken out in Mauritania while I was there (although the government denied it), locusts had invaded the entire Sahel region and, everywhere across West Africa, adults and children continued to die at a phenomenal rate of malaria, malnutrition, and dysentery. Spared cholera, I contracted malaria and amoebic dysentery in the remote north of Nigeria.

Beyond the obstacles raised by the physical circumstances, I also faced a barrier that was more subtle, and, in many cases, more deadly to my project—the network of bureaucracy. In several countries, I was nearly defeated by the requirements of permits, visas, authorization, and other aspects of officialdom. Some government authorities refused to help me—aggressively—while others simply waited for their "dash" (bribe) before processing the paperwork. Everywhere in Africa, photography is still a touchy subject: after years of exploitation, negative propaganda, and the "immortalizing" of the spirit, Africans are not only suspicious, but often reject the visual portrayal of their lives as seen through the eyes of European values.

In West Africa, it is the tradition for the newcomer to present the village chief with kola nuts. It is a ritual of hospitality and a prerequisite for any dialogue—"He who brings kola, brings life." In Nigeria, the formality includes showing one's good intentions by marking the ground with chalk. After my "acceptance," the chief would then arrange for a meeting—usually held under a baobab tree—with the village elders to discuss the reason for my being there. My interest in the walls, patterns, and lizard or crocodile relief was most often beyond comprehension. Nonetheless, the women folk would then have to be summoned through the chief's first wife, often a lengthy process. Without their final permission to be photographed at work, I could not proceed. For fear of bush fires destroying the crops, their only livelihood, women took turns sleeping in the fields for several days at a stretch to keep watch. Days—sometimes even weeks—would drift by while I waited for these women to return home. During this time—and before photography could begin—I would be granted the privilege and honor of living with the families and of being invited into their homes and their lives, of getting to know my subjects, their customs and beliefs, and of sharing their daily meals. Then, with the women in from the fields and the harvesting done, everyone would begin work on the compound. One advantage of my subject matter—the art of African woman—was that it mitigated the problems of being a woman traveling alone.

West Africa is a massive slice of a measureless continent. Hardships, loneliness, constant battles at border posts, bribery, corruption, fear, and, at times, the struggle to survive in the most exasperating circumstances were overwhelming to say the least. But when I finally reached a village and met the women there, I was accepted into their lives and into parts of their homes where not even the men are allowed. The freedom to witness and participate, to enter into the spirit and photograph, was beyond any doubt the advantage of being a woman, and, in the end, what mattered.

My relationship with the women varied from one country to another. I found that the poorer the region and the greater the struggle to survive, the more receptive and hospitable were the people. Not only were small ceremonies held in my honor at which I was presented with gifts (ranging from clay pots to guinea fowl and goats), but the women opened their hearts with natural dignity to share with me what they knew of and felt about their dying tradition—never demanding a penny. In Nigeria, the price was steep. The Igbo are an aggressive people, which I am told is the result of bitterness after a long and bloody civil war, the war of Biafra (1967–1970). This might also explain why almost all of their rich artistic tradition has disappeared. In one village, I was not allowed to photograph the shrine for spiritual or divine reasons (though it took several days to assemble the women to reach this decision). In another village, the demand was several hundred dollars. The former reason I respected, the latter saddened me deeply. Oualata once rivaled Timbuktu for trade, and its Moorish women, skilled at bargaining, demand high prices to be photographed, and then only from the back. The considerably poorer and more isolated Soninke embrace visitors warmly and share freely. Theirs is one of the few cultures in West Africa eager to protect and preserve their unrivaled artistic tradition. Unlike the art of the Ndebele, which underwent transformations through alternative building methods and the use of Western symbols and commercial paints, the vernacular art and architecture in West Africa is there one day and gone with the next rainy season. As the older generation of women die, their homes disintegrate and with them the painting. The younger women are not involved with the tradition, nor do they want to be. They are lured into the towns and cities, into a world of consumption and corruption, for what they believe is a better life than the rural hardships; many end up in slums. An exception to this trend is the women of the extremely remote areas of southern Mauritania, although since my journey, things may have changed there too. In 1989, an ethnic revolt between the Mauritanians and the Senegalese resulted in the expulsion and uprooting of thousands of people from this area.

While traveling in West Africa over three years, I had occasion to talk with many women, albeit through interpreters. Their feelings about rural life were straightforward and honest. That they should eke out an existence by growing groundnuts and yams in eroded soil or by building mud dwellings (more so decorate them) is from necessity more than choice. They would prefer to live in towns where social equality is more evident, in cinderblock houses which require less effort to maintain, and, in the name of "progress," succumb to white values. These conflicting priorities are sad but understandable.

I learned a good deal about African life: the people and nations; ugliness and beauty; brutality and tenderness; and the passage of time. I became more aware of colonies and colonization. Its effects dug deep into the spirit of all Africans, its influence generating both chaos and order. Africa is a continent of contradictions, where the real seems unreal—and the reality hopelessly sad. There were times I felt I was more a "cultural doctor" than a photographer, grappling with a terminal disease, attempting to inject a spirit of encouragement so that women might sense the validity of their dwindling traditions and move to revive them. And there were other moments I felt that my presence and interest had aroused enthusiasm for the first time in some women's lives. This was particularly noticeable in the more remote areas through the proud village chiefs under whose influence and command rural women inevitably prevail.

Whatever the reasons or causes for change, there are still—as this book testifies—women who continue to accept the struggle with exceptional resolution; who build their homes according to an ancient custom handed down through generations; who mold mud with great flexibility and discipline, despite the incredible odds. Meanwhile, one can only hope that African governments will realize the importance of combining modernization with the social and cultural life of their people. If greater effort is applied, perhaps the failing and vulnerable art of their women can be revived.

Margaret Courtney-Clarke

COMPOUND

Building in sub-Saharan Africa was, until recent years, considered "primitive." It was regarded as technological at most, in terms of materials and techniques, but more so as a product of geographical and climatic conditions. Little consideration was given to its creative distinction or aesthetic merits.

The African has always had to combine mythical and cultural practices, such as animist and Islamic ideologies, with socio-political and economic influences. The architecture of West Africa incorporates all these factors as well as the African's own concept of form and space. Together, it reflects the culture, sedentary or nomadic peoples, family, and power and wealth.

A settlement—consisting of a male head, his wives, and their offspring, and usually the sons with their families—is often isolated in its surrounding farmland. Within the settlement are a number of compounds, one for each male and for each of his wives and children. These compounds are connected by walls creating a secure and compact plan (this concept is said to have originated during slave trading). Within each compound is a dwelling for living and sleeping, covered storage areas, and detached or semi-detached dry and wet season kitchens. The dwellings may be round or rectangular, or a combination of both, depending on the region or ethnic clan. However, they always have a flat earthen roof where it is common practice for the inhabitants to sleep during the long, hot period before the rains. Social organization is formed within the framework of the compound which is an amorphous shape and can be altered to accommodate human realities—extended for a growing family or reduced when a member dies.

Building techniques are similar to those used throughout Africa: the men are responsible for the heavy construction work whereas women gather the materials and carry out the plastering. A woman plans her own living space according to the principles and customs that she brings with her from her father's settlement, such as raised sleeping platforms and structures to accommodate cooking methods. To complete her design concept, the women will then finish the wall surfaces—with the collaboration of co-wives and relatives—by applying relief work or decorative patterns which are symbolic of the female role and the world around her.

Within the settlement there is a corral for keeping animals such as goats and chickens. It is usually divided from the living area by low walls over which one strides aided by a stepping stone, or a high wall where one must use a ladder. Within the animal enclosures, tall mud granaries, with broad bases which narrow at the top and

Preceding pages: Partial view of the Kassena royal settlement on the outskirts of the village Tiébélé, Burkina Faso. Chief Aneya and his fifteen wives live in a vast complex of compounds interwoven with walls and impenetrable to the outsider. The rooftops are used for storing and drying foods as well as for sleeping during the dry season.

Opposite: The royal settlement's shebeen, *or drinking house, bearing two welcoming handshake motifs and the hourglass drum and the triangular, broken calabash patterns, was painted by Katiana Aneya.*

Opposite: It is customary for the wives in a settlement to share their views on the decoration and beauty of one another's compounds. Royal settlement. Tiébélé

Following pages: Details from two Nankani compounds, one in Sirigu, Ghana, the other in Guenon-Tipó, Burkina Faso. The triangular broken calabash pattern sets off the window and notched tree trunk ladder.

are capped with thatched roofs, are built on wooden stilts to supply ventilation and offer shade to chickens. These adobe structures, which are similar to ancestral pillars often found at compound entrances, store grain which is first dried on the roof of the dwellings. Some people also store the millet or corn in large woven baskets placed within a compound's walls. The granary is a sign of economic prestige and a symbol of family unity, and its position is at the nucleus of a settlement. Increasingly, social pressure is influencing building methods. As industrial materials become more available through wages earned in towns or cities and through the building of roads, items such as corrugated metal sheets, cinderblocks, and timber are replacing the traditional roofs, mud walls, and low tunnel-like doorways—all of which effectively keep interiors cool, dry, and safe.

Mud compounds, though not permanent, allow for considerable architectural variety and flexibility—and set in Africa's harsh landscape, they emanate great sturdiness and solidity while serving the needs of the inhabitant.

Opposite: Solid and fortress-like, this back view of the Aneriba family compound is decorated with bold V-shaped patterns, a somewhat simplified version of the tana *motif derived from local fabrics. The walls are coated with resin from the dawa-dawa tree to protect the surface from the rains. Sirigu, Ghana*

Above: Wall detail from the same compound with the triangular motif called wanzagsi, *"broken calabash"*

Above: The Kusasi settlement of regent Prince Yahya Awelinga. Painted by the late chief's wives in the customary black-and-white pattern derived from the striped loincloth, tana, *and the traditional hourglass stool,* kug. *Tilli, Ghana*

Opposite: An isolated Kassena dwelling in the rocky hills surrounding Tiébélé, Burkina Faso. Women must walk miles each day to collect water. Millet is grown in the open patches among the rocks and, when dried, the stalks and leaves are gathered for cooking fuel and livestock fodder.

Opposite: The forked wooden beam, with carved steps, allows access to the roof at all times; whereas a similar ladder indoors leads below ground level to the woman's private sanctum where she stores food and herbal medicines in clay pots. This handsome Kassena compound is the home of the Donnawanu family in the district of Navrongo-Saboro, Ghana.

Above: Dried millet hangs above the doorway of Akalem's house; like all foodstuffs above an entrance, it is a gesture of hospitality and will be served either roasted or pounded to guests. The vertical zig-zag pattern represents deer legs, togo-naga, while the bottom and top section of parallel lines crossed with diagonal lines represent furrows, gwenu. A low wall immediately inside the tunnel entrance acts as a deterrent against outsiders and prevents water from penetrating the rooms behind.

Above and opposite: After the walls have been restored with a mixture of mud and dung, white chalk signifying purity is rubbed on to smooth the surface and add highlight. The Kassena women then use coal tar mixed with sand and boiling water to paint their traditional patterns. The tar is absorbed into the mud surface and acts as an antiseptic and renders the surface water impermeable.

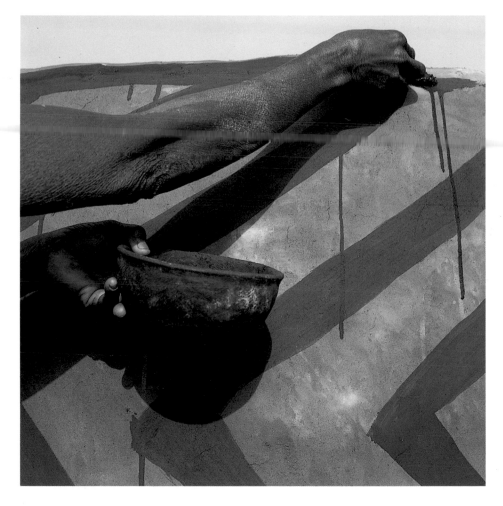

Following pages: Abolua Aberinga in the courtyard of her compound. The dipped wall in the foreground is the entrance and divides the living domain from the thatched granaries and livestock area. The roofless, dry season kitchen and the semi-covered wet season kitchen are only accessible by climbing over the far wall. The painted triangles represent the broken calabash; the flattened triangles, the calabash rope-net, both important female symbols. Sirigu, Ghana

Opposite and above: Akalem Donnawanu draws the furrow pattern on the wall of her home using coal tar.

Below: Rectilinear forms in building are not common in northern Ghana. They are said to be an Islamic import from the north. Here the women of Sirigu have adopted this outside influence and decorated the walls with traditional motifs: the handshake, agure-nuusi, *and a woven fabric,* tana.

Opposite: The wooden, forked stepladder and the low arched doorway are the most common exterior features of rural compounds throughout the upper regions of Ghana where the following photographs were taken:

Top left: Painted by Ababira Akambase

Top right: Adumpoka Atoyuure

smoking a pipe in front of her doorway decorated with a snake-relief, bohinbore

Middle left: Painted by Kapuri Awampaga, wife of the Paga chief

Middle right: Painted by Adumpoka Atoyuure. The predominant motif, calabash rope-net, wanzaana, *is divided by fine vertical zig-zags representing the wings of the vampire bat,* sisera vona.

Bottom left: Children take shelter from the midday sun.

Bottom right: From behind the subentrance, children look on at activities in the compound.

Mud is an ancient building material used virtually by all the peoples of West Africa. It is a material of relatively short durability, subject to cracking from exposure to high temperatures and eroding after heavy rains. On the other hand, mud is economical because of its availability, and highly efficient as it absorbs heat during the day and gradually releases it at night. Varying in color and consistency, mud has great plasticity, allowing the builder or decorator to produce a number of different shapes, forms, and tones. With the addition of cow dung, urine, or other binders, such as straw or slimy plant extracts, mud is molded into sturdy dwellings, often with sculptured parapet walls, staircases, and elaborate gateposts. A facade may even incorporate a colonnade or include openwork which looks out onto the compound. Mud is also used to mold or emboss decorative motifs. Dried millet or corn cobs are used to imprint wet mud for both ornamentation as well as protection from the elements. Rain water runs off these protrusions, preventing erosion of the walls. Oil residues from plants are mixed with the mud and are used to coat the wall surfaces, making them water insoluble and enhancing their color.

Mud bricks are used in some areas as opposed to the wet-mud technique, which adds layer upon layer of mud. Bricks are made by hand from a mixture of clay, sand, and water and then left to dry in the sun. In either form, mud is used to build not only the walls of a dwelling but also sitting platforms or benches, beds or resting platforms, shelving or niches to hold personal possessions, and fetish shrines—all of which create an exciting display of space integrated with the functional form of the dwelling.

Preceding pages: This spectacular compound, home of the Atoyuure family, is comprised of an outdoor cooking area, a thatched storage room, a sleeping-cum-living room for a wife, another for her young children, and the ever-present stepladder to the roof. Shea nuts are being dried on the clay floor. They will then be ground, boiled, and made into shea butter for cooking, while the residue, burima, will be used for coating the walls after decoration. Sirigu, Ghana

Opposite: A crumbling mud facade at the entrance to a Soninke compound in the village of Yaféra, Senegal

Following pages: A row of freshly restored mud houses in the village of Buanch, Mauritania

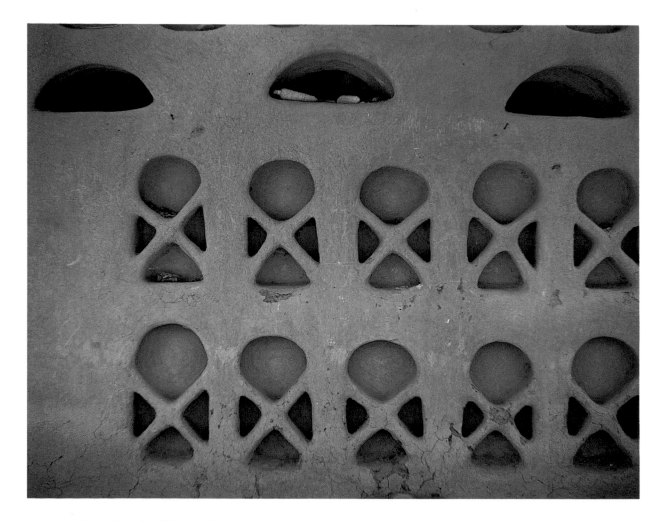

Above: Facade of a Toucouleur
home. Odobéré, Senegal

Above: A Soninke woman,
Buanch, Mauritania

The versatility of mud in form and function is evident in these examples of house facades.

Opposite: Cumba Conte spinning cotton. Hamady Ounaré, Senegal

Opposite: Entrance to an elegant Bulsa dwelling, home of the Abobyeri family. Subtle curved lines in bas-relief blend harmoniously with the warm earth tones. Millet cobs are pressed into the wet mud to create the textured wall surface. Chuchiliga-Tadem, Ghana

Above: Wall detail showing indentations of the maize cob. From a functional point of view, they diverge the path of rain water; symbolically, they represent longevity. Tiogo, Burkina Faso

*Above: One of the few remaining
flat-roofed rectangular houses
with perforated walls in
traditional style to be found
among the Soninke people living
along the Senegal River.
Ouaoundé, Senegal*

Above: The harsh and desolate living conditions in northwest Ghana are reflected in this humble yet graceful Bulsa home in Wiaga Yesobsa.

Following pages: The rectangular building with timber doors is synonymous with Islamic architecture which is fast penetrating Black Africa's Savannah region. This doorway is flanked by typical arabesque relief work in the remote settlement of Oualata, Mauritania.

*Following pages: A magnificent
compound set in the midst of a
millet field. Sirigu, Ghana*

*Opposite, top left: Wall detail
with bold criss-cross pattern
painted with vegetable dyes by
Avokbun Awelinga, a Kusasi
from Tilli, Ghana
Top right: Animal skulls are
used for spiritual and healing
rituals by a diviner, a religious
leader. Yikine, Ghana
Bottom left: An elaborate
doorway in the compound of a
Dagomba chief, decorated in
customary style with broken
porcelain plates and
enamelware. Nyankpala, Ghana*

*Bottom right: A small window
allows air to circulate while
keeping the interior cool.*

*Above: The entrance to a Grunne
compound. Ancestral shrines,*
tengani, *with chicken coops at
the base, are a prominent feature
upon which animals, usually
chickens, are sacrificed in a
ritual of ancestor worship.
Yikine, Ghana*

PAINTING

Wall painting is a much neglected facet of African art. Like the painted homes of the Ndebele and other peoples of southern Africa, this art form occurs among many ethnic groups spread across the vast area south of the Sahara. Wall art, along with body decoration, cloth dyeing, and pottery, is primarily a woman's art and is closely integrated with her domestic duties of child rearing, preparing meals, overseeing general compound activities, and participating in field labor.

It is in the dry season, after the crops have been gathered, dried, and stored in granaries, that women turn to their artistic talents. The dry season is also a time of restoring their mud houses, preparing for ceremonies, and considering future economic needs and how best to meet them with the selling of pottery and dyed cloth. Therefore, the women combine their practical day-to-day domestic responsibilities with their art. Wall painting is an accepted activity, a way of life, a joy of life. For women, the art is a natural gesture, as necessary and as incorporated in the lifestyle of these people as is walking, eating, and sleeping. Foremost, the art form is a means of beautifying the space in which they and their families spend a great deal of time, of enhancing an otherwise harsh environment. It is also a magical form of creativity, the magic coming not from its meaning or intent but from the actual act of applying the paint to the wall.

The origin of mural decoration is not clear, being a tradition handed down from mother to daughter, generation after generation, without any knowledge of what lies behind it other than the significance of certain patterns and motifs. A few older women offer the explanation of it being a result of cultural and religious influences over time, the subtle intermixture of Islamic elements with the African's needs and resources. Today, wall painting has lost much of its historical identity as West Africans are succumbing to Western values, and Christianity and Islam continue to challenge traditional beliefs. Despite overwhelming odds, what has survived—though sporadically—is the belief in community and the personal obligations to that community. Social interaction among women, especially between co-wives in a polygamous society, and their need for self-expression as well as their desire to please their husband are reasons for the art which survives today.

Throughout West Africa, decorating wall surfaces is the collective effort of several women, usually initiated by a senior wife owing to her experience or by the owner of the home whose choice of patterns reflects her identity. Other times a woman more skilled in a particular aspect of line drawing or who is especially sensitive to aesthetics may oversee the process. Before painting begins, the women must restore and replaster the walls with a mixture of mud and cow dung. The surfaces are smoothed by hand, using a brew of dung and urine, in itself creating a subtle pattern. Organic materials are used for both the paints—in the form of indigenous pigments—and the tools, made from plants or feathers. Flat colors or relief work, or a combination of the two, are applied to the wall in a variety of patterns and motifs.

Unlike the building methods, carried out by the men and tending to be less innovative, there is an individual style to surface finishing for the women. The most common practice is to use earth pigments painted onto a freshly plastered surface, often layer upon layer. This layering slows the drying process of the paints, as well as cracking, thus creating a smudged effect, an "indistinctness" between pattern and surface. Since the patterns reflect the world around her, they illustrate the idea that "dwellings and their inhabitants are in fact an indistinguishable ideological as well as physical unit" (*Arts in Ghana*, 1977). On the other hand, the Soninke women of Mauritania mainly decorate the interior walls of their homes. Bold geometric shapes in muted colors are painted on dry walls, resembling hung art, and are not integrated in the architectonic structure. Similarly, the Igbo women of Nigeria use sharply drawn line motifs to communicate their status in their community; and somewhere between all the styles, the Soninke of Senegal produced an art form (now extinct) which embraced bas-relief with geometry, geometry with architecture, and color with relief work. Besides obvious regional differences in wall painting, there are other differences as well. Young women when they marry leave their own family settlements to join their husband's. They take with them methods and established practices learned from their mothers which they then incorporate with those of their new family. These younger artists may apply fresh solutions to customary methods, despite a basic lexicon of descriptive images and design formulas.

The lifespan of painted walls—subject to disintegration—is not intended to be permanent. Rather, the walls are recreated each year to celebrate or announce new events and to permit women to partake in a communal or social activity.

Preceding page: Soninke women, Bidia Gandega, Fenda Gandega, Silla Camara, and Manthi Gandega decorate a wall in the Gandega family compound. Though noncompetitive, Silla leads the group by virtue of experience in a friendly and informal atmosphere. Djajibinni, Mauritania

Above: Using a spoon, Silla Camara spontaneously outlines an abstract design, jabande.

Opposite: Like all house decoration in West Africa, painting is a communal endeavor in Soninke villages. During the unfolding of a work, suggestions are made through flowing discussions as well as constructive criticism.

Opposite: Silla Camara applies fo khoule—*a paste of ground white limestone and water—to the mud wall,* tagaye, *of her house. Traditionally, only red earth,* fo doumbe, *black,* fo bine, *and white were used. In more recent years, the younger generation of women have added washing blue,* boula; *yellow,* makka; *and intermediate shades of pink and purple.*

Above: Before starting the next panel, Silla takes a break to nurse her child, while Fenda adds the final touches to their morning's work.

Above: Soninke women use only their hands and fingers to apply the earth pigments obtained from the Senegal river area.

Opposite: In the isolated desert settlements of southern Mauritania, Soninke women divide a wall surface into panels before painting purely abstract, geometric designs to create a vibrant rhythm along the flat surface.

Opposite and above:
Dioncounda, Assa, and Dianna
Camara decorate a wall for a
festive occasion using a zig-zag
pattern, learned from their
mothers, although its origin or
meaning is unknown to them.
Buanch, Mauritania

Oualata, in the extreme southwest of Mauritania, was from medieval times until the eighteenth century a major cultural center of the Sahara, rivaled only by Timbuktu. Its citizens, principally Moors, were traders who traveled to North Africa as well as south of the Sahara to Guinea, Ivory Coast, and Nigeria. As a result, their culture was influenced by many different peoples with whom they came into contact. Oualata is a cultural island with a unique building tradition enhanced by the splendid wall decoration of the women. No other Moorish settlement in Mauritania bears remotely similar features.

Unlike other parts of West Africa, wall decoration is not necessarily carried out by the home owner, and never by women of noble families. Rather the art is created by wives of the working class—the blacksmith and laborers—and by Black servants.

Different methods and color combinations are used depending on the location of the wall. The exterior facades which are plastered with a deep, red-brown earth are painted with bold, white lines interspersed with chain-like patterns and, on either side of the doorway, motifs are engraved or molded. Staircases, archways, and columns are outlined in white creating a unified space. Interior rooms are entirely whitewashed with a mixture of clay and water. Using her finger, a woman then applies a dark red earth color, abundant in the area, to create intricate filigree decoration. The number of motifs on the walls and around doors and windows varies according to the use of the space or room. Servant quarters and utility rooms, such as cooking areas, bear simple designs in light ocher shades, whereas the principal rooms, such as the main bedroom, will be elaborately decorated in red. It is in the courtyards that the women of Oualata reveal surprisingly rich mural decoration.

The insular and cloister-like life of Oualata women prevents the outsider from learning much about the meaning of their art. They offer little explanation other than their desire to make their homes attractive.

Opposite: Miriam Boughi in the courtyard of her home. The relief-work on the wall was made by cutting out pieces of mud with a knife and filling in the spaces with colored earth pigments.

Opposite: Lumlass mint Ahmed applies red pigments to mud relief. She is considered an apprentice and is learning the art of decoration from an older and more experienced woman.

Above: Izi Sass, a daughter of the mayor of Oualata, sits beneath a typical decoration. Named "mother with thighs," the design is derived from a symbol representing part of a woman's thigh which is repeated in infinite combinations. Patterns are named after parts of the body, actions or postures, and Arabic letters.

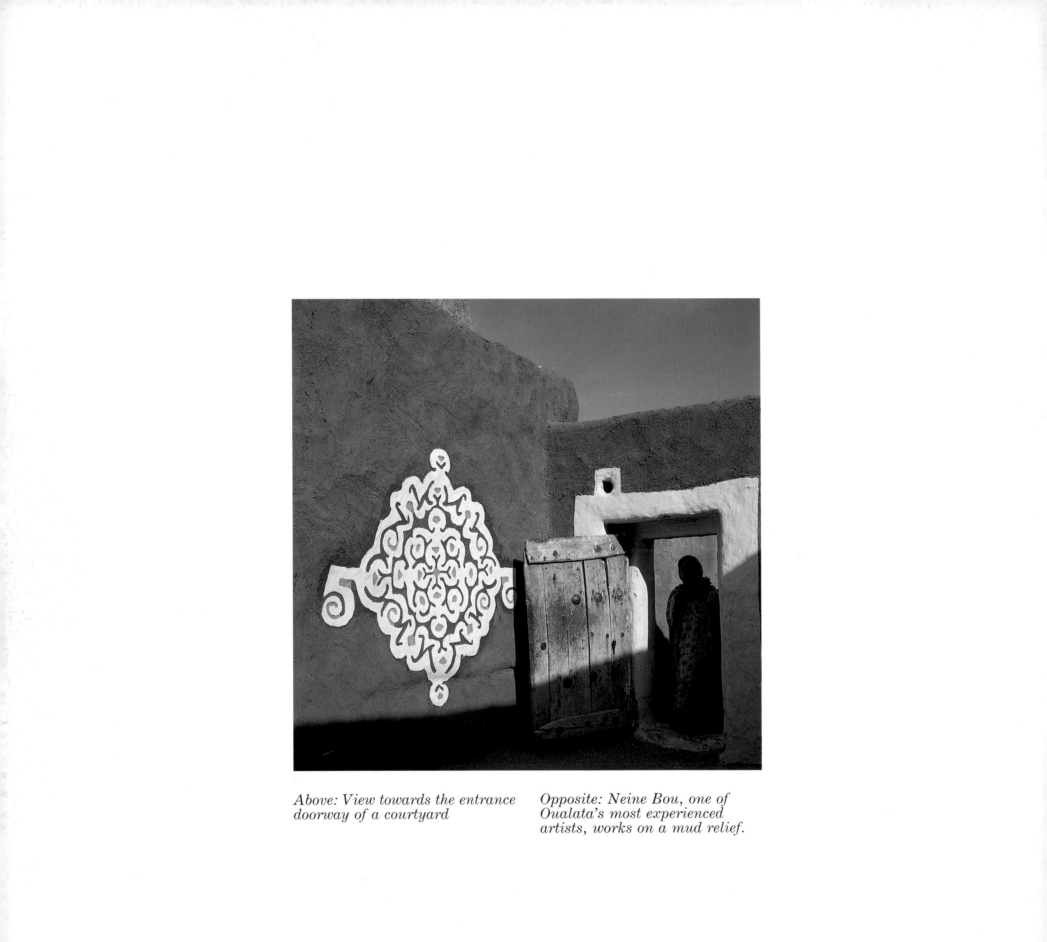

*Above: View towards the entrance
doorway of a courtyard*

*Opposite: Neine Bou, one of
Oualata's most experienced
artists, works on a mud relief.*

Opposite: Young women learn from Neine Bou through observation as she skillfully demonstrates the art.

Above: Neine Bou, using a knife to remove surplus mud, creates a filigree-like design. The wealthier the family, the more intricately decorated are the interior and exterior walls of their homes. However, the inhabitants do not decorate their own homes, rather it is done by the wives of the laborers and Black servants.

Above: Ghudeije mint Mohamed, using her finger, applies a deep, red-brown color to a whitewashed interior wall.

Opposite: Nany mint Sass uses a combination of motifs representing parts of the body to create a decorative element around a doorway. The Koran forbids figurative representation of living beings; therefore, ideograms symbolize a form.

Above: In their wall decoration, the women of Oualata use only their fingers to apply clay pigments combined with gum arabic which acts as an adhesive.

Opposite: Detail of an interior wall with arabesques and spirals suggesting human figures, punctuated by lines and geometric patterns

Uli can be many things. Foremost, it is an art form which characterizes a style. A woman's art, *uli* is used in both body and wall painting and shares common motifs despite the disparity of surfaces and materials used. The *uli* medium is a liquid extract from the pod or fruit of a variety of trees. When used to draw particular designs on the skin for a specific ceremony, the liquid causes blisters to rise which last for several days. The motifs created by this swelling are called *uli*; in the same manner, these motifs and patterns, when applied to mud surfaces using clay pigments, are also called *uli*.

The function of body or wall *uli* is to beautify the person or home, a manifestation through which Igbo women assert their identities as individuals and as a clan. Regrettably, this painting tradition is rare these days as Nigerians have rapidly opted for Western culture and comforts. What remains of *uli* varies from village to village, or clan to clan, each woman applying her own individuality, although the designs, symbols, and techniques are basically the same throughout Igboland. Women (and men) are painted for numerous reasons: to distinguish themselves from others, to take an *Ozo* title of power and authority, to communicate, and for maiden festivals, wedding ceremonies, and burials.

Uli patterns are named after objects, animals, plants, or the activities of women. The most frequent motifs are from the plant world, such as cassava leaves, seed pods, yams, and the flowers of fruit. The kola nut, a symbol of peace and hospitality, is well-represented in its various split stages.

A motif can represent the object or pattern for which it is named (a cooking pot or textile design), or it can signify something entirely abstract, such as reconciliation after a quarrel. Others are invented purely as a design element. There are motifs for the old and young, the thin and fat, as well as for different parts of the body and for different occasions. Most body art, however, consists of lines: concave-convex lines, thin tapering lines, curving lines with hook shapes, delicate lines accentuated by more curves, rows of vertical lines, or flat areas punctuated by triangles, circles, or dots. There are thousands of motifs and patterns which comprise the *uli* style. Whatever the meaning, *uli* is a woman's reaction to the Igbo way of life.

Opposite: Detail of uli *used in the decoration of a shrine. Abatete, Nigeria*

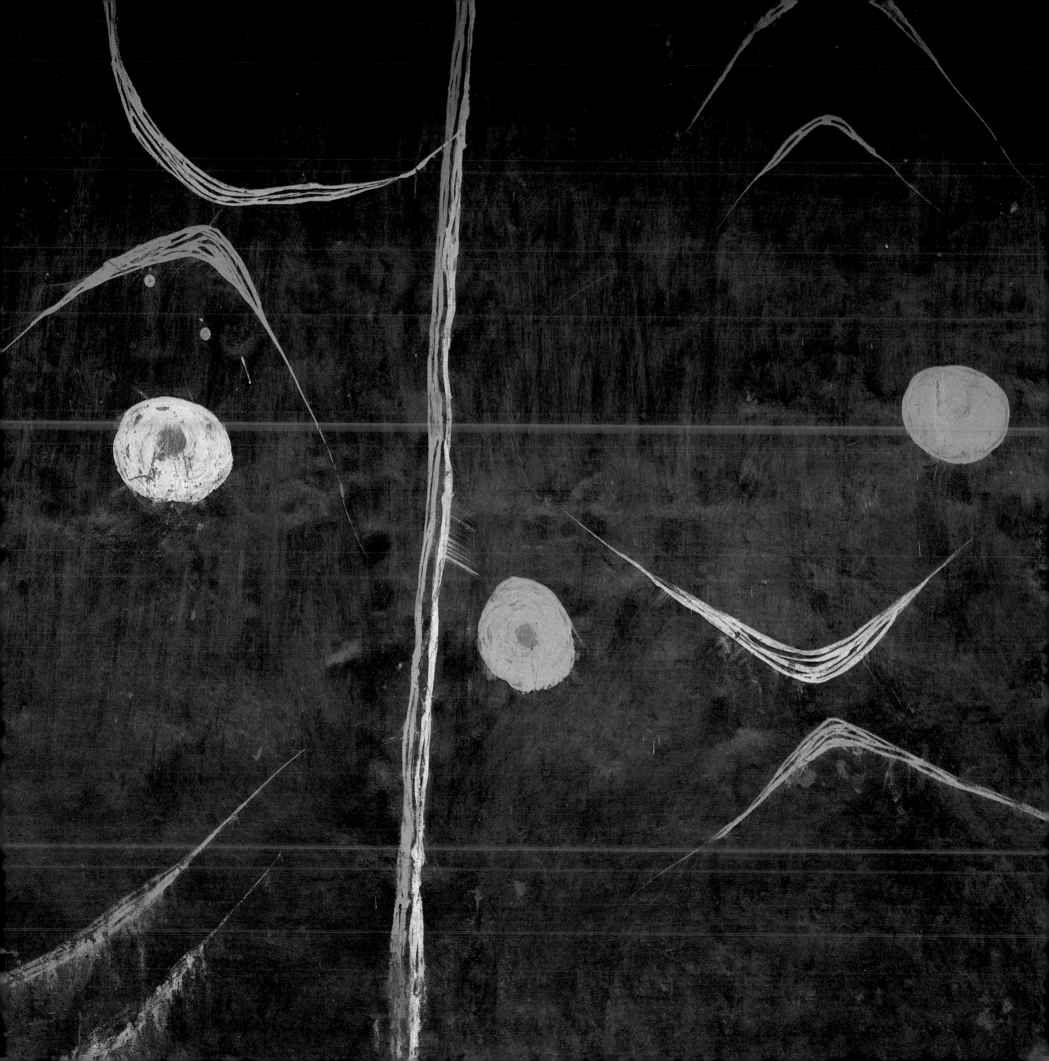

Opposite: A village community shrine painted by Igbo women in Abatete, Nigeria

Above: Detail of painted abstract motifs related to uli

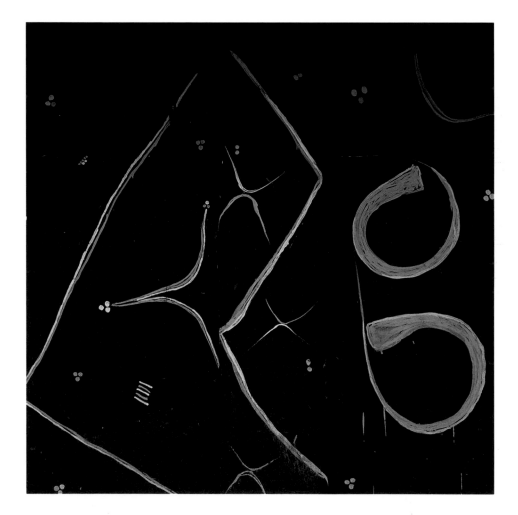

Above and opposite: Details of painted uli *patterns, celebrating the taking of an Ozo title, on the walls of the Okeke family home. Omini-Uke, Nigeria*

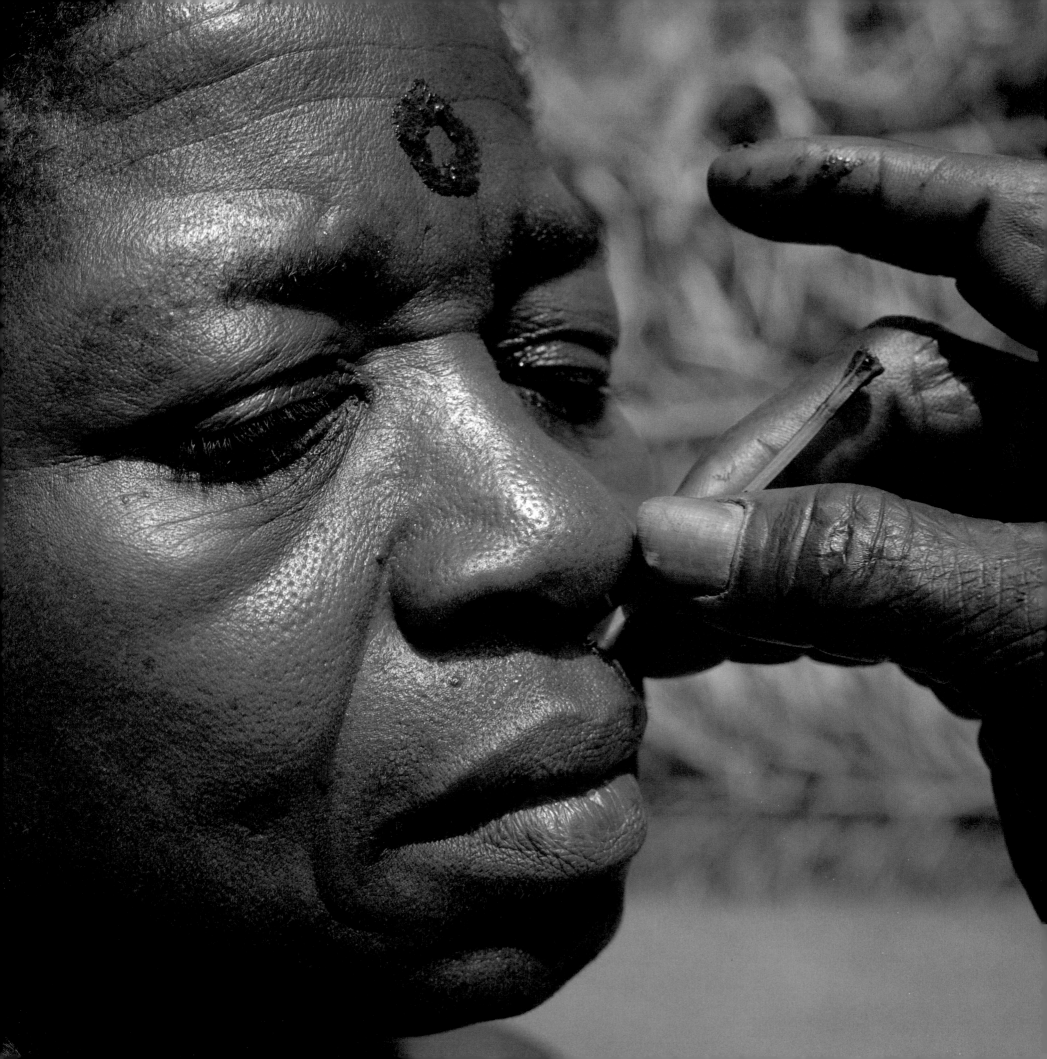

Opposite: Uli *is painted on the face of Ogbungwa. In* uli, *body painting and wall painting share common motifs despite the contrasting surfaces and materials used. Olido, Nigeria*

Above: The uli *line pattern,* nwanyioma, *signifies the person is considered "good" by other women in her community.*

Above: When a woman quarrels with a fellow woman, the one who settles the argument, the "free" one, paints vertical lines on her chest.

Opposite: The seeds of a fruit, locally called the uli *fruit, are crushed and the resulting clear liquid is applied to the body with a fine piece of wood. This blisters the skin, creating a raised dark pattern, for the duration of a ceremony.*

In Nigeria today, social pressure has caused many of its people to scorn the traditional mud house with thatched roof, considering such housing inferior and reeking of impoverishment. With the exception of the public or domestic shrine and the *Obi*, the meeting place and center of the family life found in the domestic compounds, little remains of indigenous architecture and less so of wall decoration. For both the shrine and the *Obi*, the decorators are the Igbo women whose motivation is to achieve an aesthetic rather than a symbolic or meaningful content.

A wall is usually divided into rectangular panels. One panel will contain bold representations of animals or human figures, another may have abstract geometric designs related to women's activities, and another will reveal groups of organic motifs (*uli*), widely spaced apart and on an overall dark background. By using a variety of design concepts, the artist brings a sense of excitement to her composition as well as a certain measure of tension.

The basic colors used for mural painting in Nigeria are black, white, yellow, and red, with washing blue as a supplementary color. Colors are seldom mixed and are used to create well-defined outlines, unlike the soft or blurred colors used in Ghana or Burkina Faso. These areas of distinctly sharp colors are set off by the use of fine juxtaposed and superimposed lines or curves with twists, airy dots, and other "suspended" designs, adding a touch of joyful energy.

The most common motifs drawn on the family shrine are animals, either whole or in part, and which are often symbolic of human characteristics. Lizards and crocodiles, often difficult to distinguish from each other on the walls, are popular subjects. The python is sacred among certain Igbo clans and is therefore well-represented, either coiled or slithering across the wall with a frog in its mouth.

Opposite: Yellow chalk-like pigment, edo, is a primary color in wall painting and is found near water throughout West Africa. In Nigeria, it is applied as a paste to the body both for decorative and medicinal purposes. During the celebration held for a newborn child, edo, believed to protect against measles, is rubbed onto the skin.

Following pages: A group of Igbo women decorating the facade of a public shrine. Such public cult "houses" are associated with the unseen gods and are magnificently embellished for annual rituals. Roughly twenty women took part in the overall decoration, led by several older and more experienced artists who contributed a particular motif, either abstract and geometric or pictorial. Nri, Nigeria

*Opposite, top left: An Igbo
woman paints a cooking pot, ite,
symbolic of her domestic role,
amidst rays of the sun.
Top and bottom right: Ogalu, a
pattern derived from
scarification
Bottom left: Adding the final
touches to a rowing oar, amala.
Four rays of the sun, anyanwu,
represent emissaries sent by the
deity four days of the week,
signifying four market days.*

*Above: In a war between Igbo
families in Nigeria, daughters
settle the feud. The python, eke,
is the symbol for daughter;
hence, it is never killed. When a
woman dies, a python is
sacrificed to the deity.*

Above: A wall surface is divided into vertical panels which bear alternating abstract patterns from uli *with images from the everyday life of the Igbo people— a musical instrument, a python, and a crocodile.*

Opposite: Nwunna from Nri was attracted to the Western blouse she wears because of its resemblance to the traditional diamond-shaped motif used in scarification, ogalu.

Above: Luciana Azaaya paints a snake and lizard relief on the wall above the grinding platform. The snake, wobig-ziifo, is highly revered in some Grunne compounds. The lizard, bang-doo, is "always around where humans live." Zaare, Ghana

*Above: Anapaoka Ayeti assists
her daughter-in-law by drawing
the outline of the calabash
rope-net,* zaalenga. *Red paint
from dawa-dawa pods has been
mixed with mud and dung to
brighten the overall tone.*

Opposite: A remarkable compound and home of Asokwine, the first wife of Chief Aneriba Zure of Sirigu, Ghana. Nankani compounds are not only influenced by climatic or social factors, they are an integral part of the people's day-to-day life, the core of their existence.

Above: Atogomtoya Aneriba smoothes the mud around the traditional semi-circular door with a stone, a method known as saase in Nankam. The vertical, scalloped motif denotes an old woman's hairstyle, pognya-gingesi, and the flattened triangles represent the calabash rope-net. In the corner, the V-shaped pattern is a sign of welcome to visitors.

Above: Asokwine clutches the roof wall while making indentations in the wet mud surface with a rounded stone.

Opposite: Each woman carries out a different process of filling in, outlining, polishing, or line drawing, although Asokwine, the home owner, directs the communal effort.

Opposite: Amina Azaaba, a Nankani, works on a relief made of mud and cow dung. A human figure next to a walking stick represents the house owner, yidaana. *The walking stick,* dogolongo, *symbolizes the authority of the family head, the one who maintains peace in the compound. Kandiga, Ghana.*

Left: Emil Amingo-Etigo, wife of Chief Kandiga-Naba, prepares black pigment.

Although mural painting is very rare nowadays in Burkina Faso—one of the world's poorest countries—in the remote surroundings of Zecco, the Wenna family maintains their Nankani tradition with extraordinary vigor. Above: the altars in the foreground are used for sacrificing chickens to the gods. Opposite: Biloa Wenna paints a chicken, a remnant of pagan idolatry.

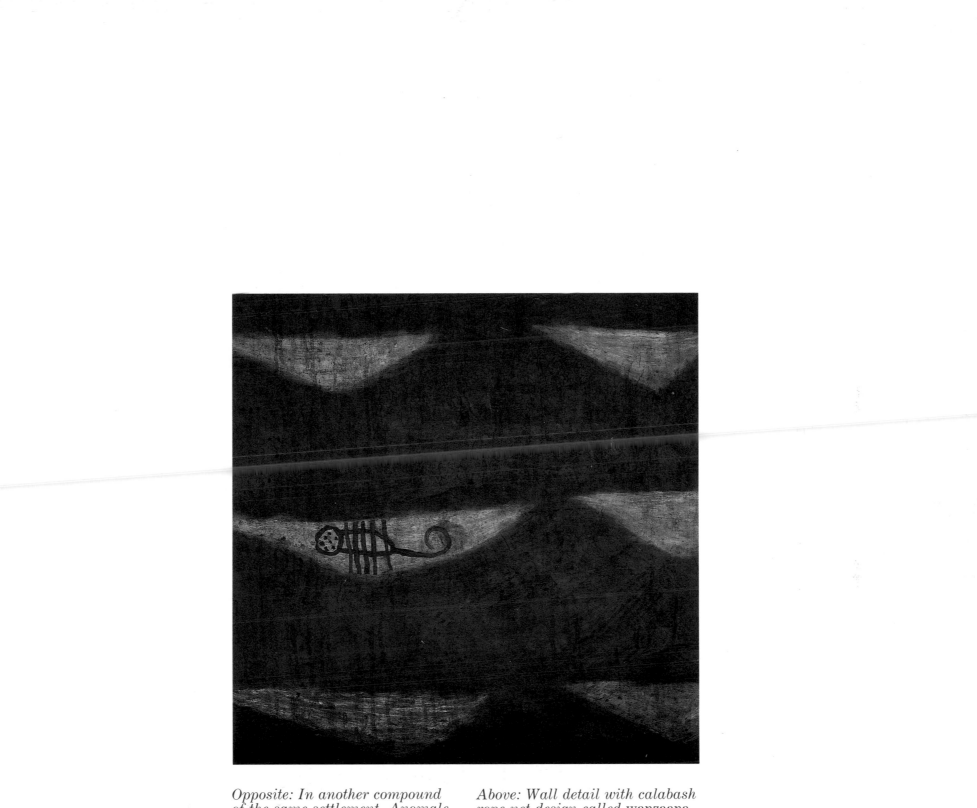

Opposite: In another compound of the same settlement, Anomale Wenna, who does not know how to paint, contributes to the work at hand by grinding pigments, collecting water, and gathering dung.

Above: Wall detail with calabash rope-net design called wanzaana. *A scorpion,* nanga, *punctuates the wall, a warning to children not to play with one.*

Above: Detail of the finished wall with gurubogoro *and* piligiyeta, *a pattern taken from local fabric.*

Opposite: Gampoko Wenna confidently divides the round wall surface into vertical lines, then adds a V-shaped line to create the handshake, gurubogoro.

Opposite: *Using dried grass as a brush*, soo, *Biloa Wenna fills in the outlined design with a blood-red earth pigment*, gare.

Above: *Unlike the Nankani in Sirigu, Ghana, their sisters across the border in Burkina Faso use brighter colors with a spontaneous freedom that causes the patterns to dance.*

Pottery is a domestic activity confined to the compound and, unlike wall painting, is of considerable economic importance. Women sell pots at local markets or use them to barter for food, clothing, or other commodities. Within the family compound, pots are used for cooking and collecting and storing water, while those with numerous holes are used for steaming pounded grains or smoking meat. Like halved calabashes, or gourds, they are also used as serving vessels or eating utensils. Producing pots necessitates several stages of activity from the preparation of the clay—usually done by young girls so that they become familiar with the medium—to the complex system of firing without kilns. Since all clay pots are made by hand in Africa, the techniques usually employed are either the coiled- or pulled-methods. In the coiled-method long strands of clay are coiled into the desired form, while in the pulled-method, the clay is pulled up and shaped. Both involve great skill which the women say often requires twenty years to perfect. Some women add a touch of colored earth pigment to the clay before molding or engrave the wet vessel with line decorations to enhance its appearance. Still others apply figurative motifs in relief work.

It is interesting to note that most clay pots made in West Africa have rounded bases. Contrary to Western thinking, these pots are said to be easier to carry on the head. A grass hoop or a cloth twisted into a ring is used for seating it on the head. While for cooking or storage, stones placed around a fire or a ring of conical mud structures built on the floor offer support.

Over and above the economic value of pottery, a certain number of traditional beliefs and rituals are attached to the significance of making and owning pots. Areas where clay is found are sometimes associated with ancestors and must be "bestowed" by a priestess. Ritual pots are used for making sacrifices to the gods, and pots used for funeral rites are elaborate "sculptures" bearing portraits of the deceased. Also, sacrifices are made before certain pots are fired, such as those used for storing medicinal herbs. Among some female potters, pregnant or menstruating women are prohibited from participating in the art. Such beliefs and social taboos emphasize the importance of pottery as a woman's activity and help to protect this social and economic preoccupation from outside competitors.

Opposite: Fine line detail is skillfully applied to a clay urn used for burning incense. Oualata, Mauritania

Following pages: Clay pots displayed at the weekly market are painted by village women from the environs of Kaédi, Mauritania.

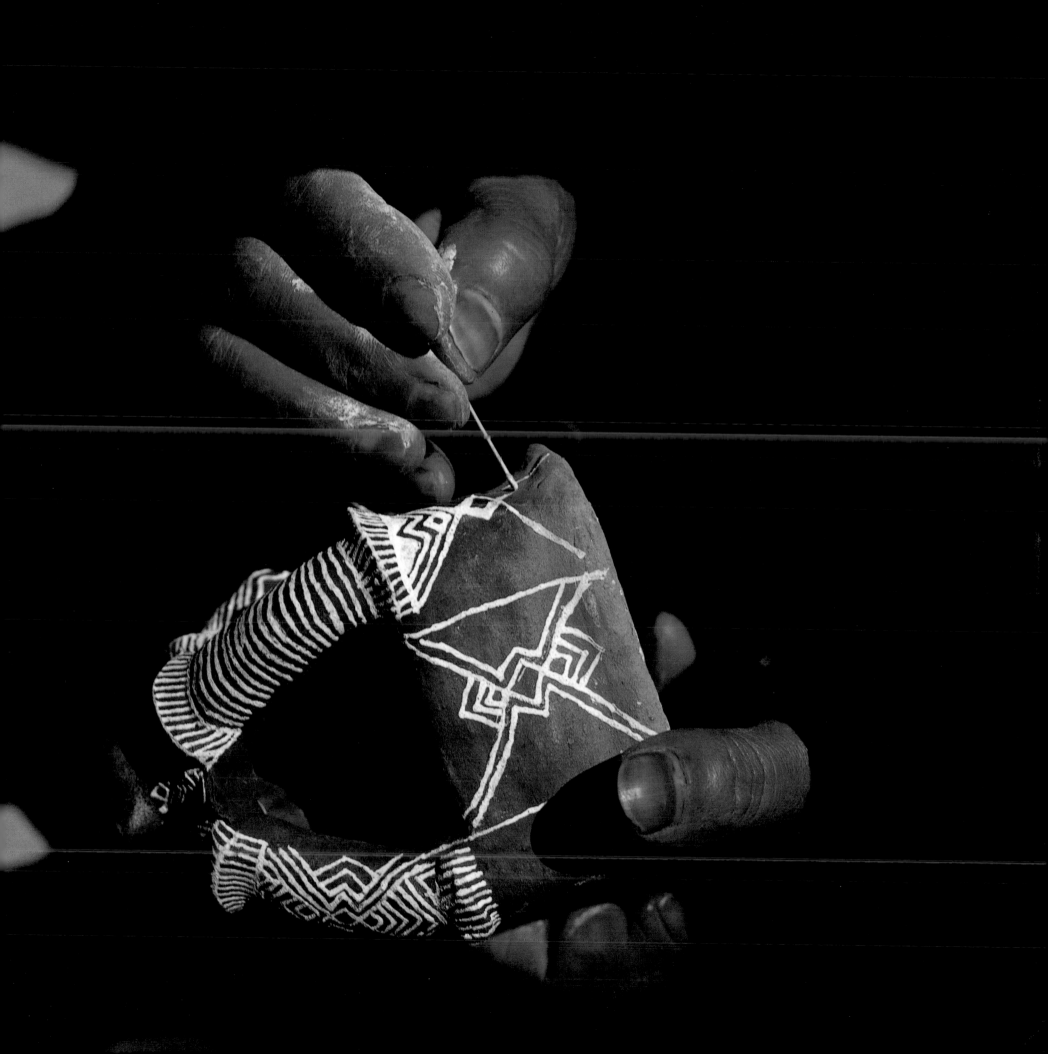

Opposite: Using the coiled-method, Rosa Satu produces a clay pot at her home in the Diola village of Oussouye, Senegal.

Above: Mah Dembele, a Bambara woman, molds a large clay pot to sell at the market. Kalabougou, Mali

*Above and opposite: Awe Bayira
and Kojigi Yire apply figurative
reliefs to their clay pots before
polishing the surface with a
chunk of white clay.
Guenon-Tipo, Burkina Faso*

Opposite: A semi-sunken den piled high with clay pots containing food, spices and medicinal herbs. In the foreground, a relief molded in the shape of the female sex organ serves as a support for the cooking pot. The small opening in the roof emits smoke and allows air circulation during the dry season. Tiébélé, Burkina Faso

Left: Decorated clay pots and a rope-net holding calabash bowls and plates, home of Akanjaglie Kwame. Wiaga, Ghana

Following pages: Interior detail of the grinding-cum-storage room belonging to Kusoubayiga Aneya from Tiébélé, Burkina Faso. A stepladder beyond the low wall takes one beneath groundlevel, where, through another low tunnel door, is a second chamber (see page 134).

Opposite: The diga *or "woman's dwelling space" defines her personal realm. A low curved wall connected to the entrance provides a platform for a large pot for storing water or groundnuts. Above is a semicircular serrated edge or sideboard whose rounded mud notches support piles of clay pots. Navrongo-Saboro, Ghana*

Above: A simple diga, *home of Agere Abahe. The size and quality of pots and calabashes which are related to incised wall patterns reflect a woman's ability to support a family, her status, prestige and reproductive powers. Yikine, Ghana*

Bogolan fini *translated literally from Bambara means "mud cloth painting." It is a unique and time consuming art through which women in the outlying areas of Ségou, Mali, have sought to express their creativity. Handwoven by men, cotton* fabrics are dyed, using abstract patterns, by women who wear them as wraparound clothing. The cloth is spread on the ground and a design is drawn with a toothbrush using a dark liquid made from boiling the bark of the wolo tree and the*

leaves of the n'golama tree. It is then left to dry in the sun. The cloth is washed before a coating of gray-black mud is added on top of the yellow-brown pattern. This process is repeated two more times: mud painting, drying, washing, until the final pattern is pitch black. (More recently, commercially sold fabrics found in markets are grayish in tone, shortcut versions in which only one or two applications of mud have been made). During the process, a spillover onto the background

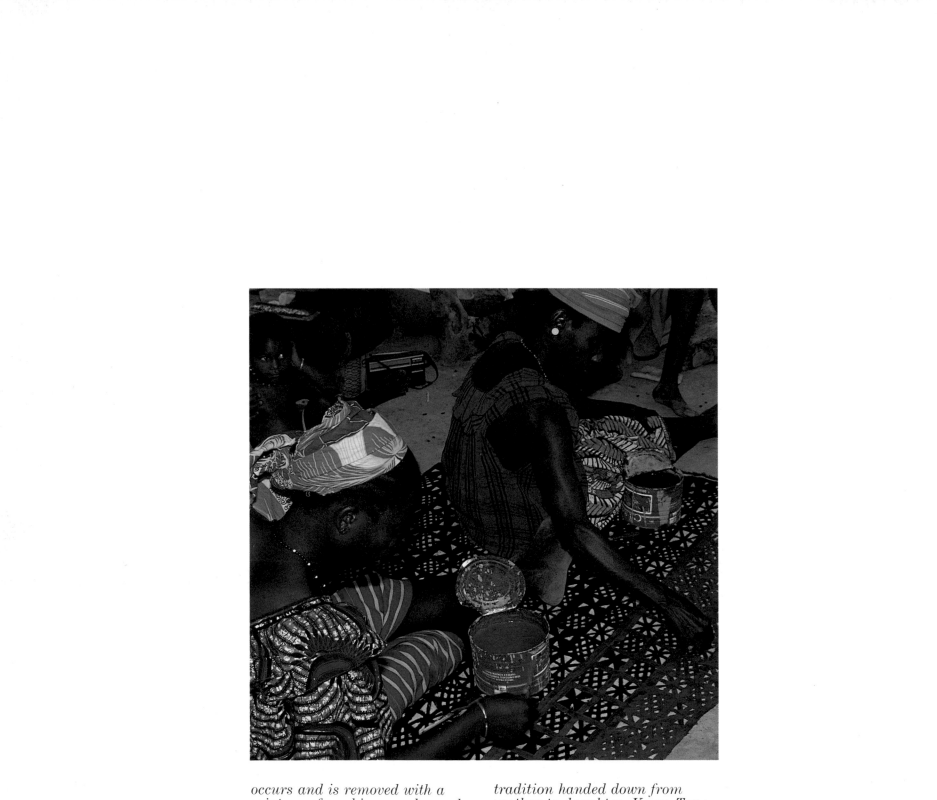

occurs and is removed with a mixture of washing powder and bleach. After a final wash, the fabric is ready to be worn or sold. Bogolan fini *is said to have originated in the village of Farako, Mali (where these photographs were taken) and is a* tradition handed down from mother to daughter. Komo Tene, wearing a white blouse, is the leader of the village group, assisted by Gneko Kembele and Oumou Kanouté, and has taught women in other villages this exceptional art.

Mural painting throughout West Africa varies considerably, from the arabesques of Oualata and the colorful abstracts of the Soninke to the brilliant representational patterns of the Igbo and the muted earth tones of the Nankani and Kassena. However, one factor is common to all—the materials used. They are all indigenous pigments: local soils or clay in different hues mixed with animal dung or plant dyes. Even washing blue, which was imported by colonials at the turn of the century, is now considered by many women indigenous and is used as a complementary color.

Opposite: Red, black, and ocher soils, abundant throughout Africa, are ground into a fine powder and then mixed with water to form a paste.

Above: Animal dung and urine are used as a binder with earth for plastering walls and with color pigments for painting. For smoothing, painting, and engraving wall surfaces, women mostly use their hands; however, other tools include stones, feathers, grass, chips of broken calabashes, and corn cobs.

149

The meaning of colors varies from region to region, or compound to compound. Chalk to some women signifies happiness and success in the family, while to others the whiteness means purity. The Kusasi women in Ghana use black for "dark days of suffering" when food is scarce, and red when someone dies (said to originate from periods of tribal war and slavery), whereas other women use red simply to brighten the decoration. In Nigeria, red is revered and called aja-nwamuo, *"sand, son of spirit."*

Preceding pages: The different methods of preparing colors and glazes used in wall painting. Some people grind leaves to use as a color, while others mix leaves with black pigment to use as a glaze; shea nuts are ground and the residue, which is left to settle in an open pit, is used to coat the walls; and one of the many black substances used is black oxide, extracted from used batteries.

Above and opposite: Painting is a communal activity. After the rains, women gather in the shade of a compound and discuss what colors to use, who shall gather what materials, and who shall walk to market—often miles away. Those who don't participate in the painting, grind colors on flat stones or with a mortar and pestle.

MOTIFS

Wall decoration is a social activity which allows the West African woman to interact with other women. The motif which is an extension of wall decoration conveys something about the individual woman, either an object, event, or belief familiar to her world or—in the case of a figurative form—about the person or animal represented. Motifs are either figurative or non-figurative though often the two are combined. Non-figurative patterns are often used to simulate skin texture on figurative representations of snakes, crocodiles, or lizards—three of the most depicted forms from the animal world. The meaning behind animals, insects, or birds portrayed on a compound wall varies from clan to clan.

In some compounds, certain animals are considered sacred. Among the Kassena women, the python was once used to guard a newborn baby while the mother was at work in the fields; today, the python image is still used as a symbol of protection. For other women, the python merely provides decorative variation in its various poises. For the Nankani, the criss-cross pattern *bohinbore* is named after a type of snake depicted by a mud-relief bulge around the opening of the almost semi-circular door. It is said to protect the inhabitant of the dwelling.

A particular compound will revere and depict a crocodile if it inhabits a sacred river. A common lizard may be painted on a flat surface, whereas another type which kills baby chickens (a revered animal) may be "sacrificed and taken as a god" and consequently represented in more complex three-dimensional relief. And a dove painted by a Boasi woman is said to "send a message to god" when something worries her.

The Kusasi women apply simple, bold criss-crosses to the walls of their homes which are enriched by figurative depictions of animals or human figures. No meaning is attached beyond an attempt to make their homes beautiful. Amongst the Igbo women the process of creating beauty depends on the woman's ability to transform figurative into non-figurative motifs, called *uli*. The latter, usually from the plant world, are applied to the human body or a figurative form from the animal world painted on the wall, such as a yam beetle painted with *uli* motifs on its back. It is a complex process of the mind which has nothing to do with rites or mysticism but rather an attempt to combine nature with Igbo culture.

The motif of the rope-net used for hanging calabashes is called *zaalenga* (meaning net) by some women, and *wanzaana* (translated literally means to hold a calabash) by other women of the same clan. Likewise, the "handshake" pattern can be seen literally as a clasping of hands or interpreted symbolically as "a greeting." In either case, it signifies peace and unity. Moreover, what may appear in one clan to be the identical motif of another's can denote entirely different subjects and meanings. A horizontal scalloped design represents a canoe to Igbo women while to a Nankani, a vertical scalloped motif represents a hair style for old women, *pognya-gingesi*.

With the exception of the abstract geometric patterns created by the Soninke women, most women in West Africa name their patterns or motifs for objects familiar to their domestic world: a cooking pot, a fish net, hourglass drums, chicken feet, weaving patterns, traditional loincloth patterns, or, the most common, a triangular motif representing a broken calabash. Whatever the origin or meaning, wall or body motifs spark curiosity as much as they communicate information. They are a woman's reponse to the world around her and, above all, adorn her home, enhancing an otherwise cheerless landscape.

Across the following pages Nankani women develop the crocodile motif, ebiga, *on a wall in the Atoyuure family compound. Sirigu, Ghana*

Opposite: Detail of two crocodiles, head to head, with a frog, kampone, *between them. Cowrie shells,* ligipelsi, *have been used for eyes.*

Following pages: View of the settlement which is divided by low walls into compounds and subcompounds for each wife. These are situated around the central animal enclosure, nandoni, *which also houses tall, mud granaries or silos,* baare. *Adumpoka splashes on a reddish clay,* zigmolgo, *mixed with cow urine, while Asaamaligo outlines the crocodile relief before the surface dries.*

Opposite and above: After a fluid mixture of cow dung and urine is splashed on the wall, Abolua Aberinga and Adumpoka smear it across the surface.

Opposite: Various stages of
applying cow dung and red and
black pigments before smoothing
the surface with a stone

Above: The final "scales" being
added to a crocodile

Above: The broken calabash pattern, wanzagsi, *is painted as a background to the crocodile relief.*

Opposite: Adumpoka and Asaamaligo polish the mural with pieces of white clay, kugpela, *to soften the harsh outlines, merging the pattern with the surface.*

Following pages: Detail of a large mural painted by Veronica Nabilia in 1973. The entire work incorporates three crocodiles: a male and female separated by a crocodile with two heads representing a god of the land and pond. Above them a female python meets a male python— Adam and Eve. The crocodiles "swim" amidst broken calabash motifs; beneath, the hourglass design represents a pestle used for crushing sheat nuts. Tiébélé, Burkina Faso

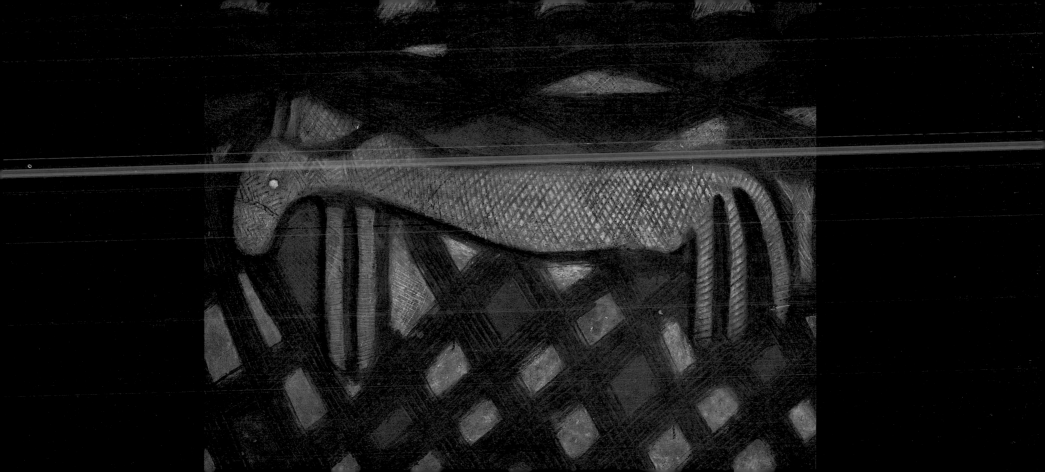

Preceding pages: Wall details from the interior of the Roman Catholic mission in Sirigu, painted in 1972 by twenty Kassena women, depicting two snakes, wafo, and a bush cow, goo-nafo

Above: A faded relief of camels and a human figure by the late Mari Kabuga from the remote settlement of Boungou, Burkina Faso

Opposite: Wall detail of Apoku Akurugu's interpretation of a man, a camel, and a beetle. Zebilla, Ghana

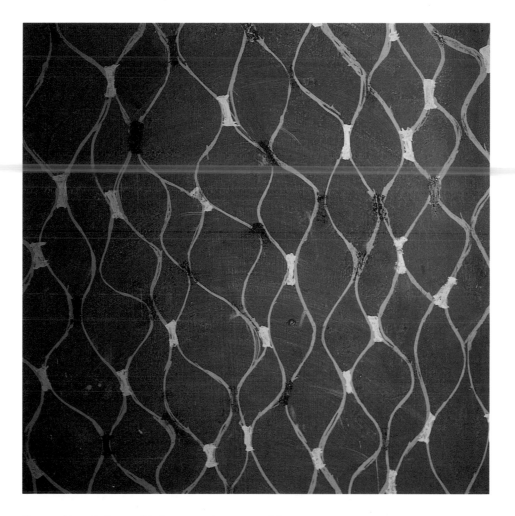

Opposite: A beautiful example of an uli pattern applied to a figurative form, a yam beetle. Nri, Nigeria

Above: Delicate lines create a rhythmic pattern depicting a knotted-string fishnet. Nri, Nigeria

Above and opposite: A panel of schematic representations of the Igbo peoples daily life, including a yam beetle with uli *motifs on its back and, in the triangle above, a double gong,* ogene. *A series of narrow vertical panels to the right bear abstract patterns derived from (left to right) a ritual cloth,* akwa-nka; *another type of cloth called* kpom-kpom; *and a scarification pattern,* ogalu.

Abstract geometric patterns used by the Soninke in Mauritania are named in French and have no meaning other than the literal translation. Opposite: Detail of an interior wall painted by Djeynaba Cisse. Buanch, Mauritania

Above: Detail of a wall incorporating the sun and the star-and-moon emblems of Mauritania (also of Islam). Painted by Fenda Gandega from the village of Djajibinni Gandega

Above: A calabash rope-net, zaalenga, *hangs from the ceiling before a wall on which Agere Abahe has painted the rope-net motif. This pattern is the most commonly used female symbol. Yikine, Ghana*

Opposite: The walking stick, dibega, *denotes authority and is painted on the wall of an old man's home, usually the head of the family. The artist Anapoaka Ayeti is a Grunne from Zaare, Ghana.*

Above and opposite: The wall of a rare rectangular house with roof terrace is decorated with broad stripes and circles—the tana *pattern derived from a local fabric—and a chain of "people clasping hands," a simplified handshake design,* agure-nuusi, *by Asokiwine Avoknore. Sirigu, Ghana*

*Following pages: This bold
motif, inspired by the triangular
loincloth traditionally worn by
men and women, was painted by
the late Asekulya Adongo.
Zaare, Ghana*

INTERIORS

The remote villages on the edge of the Sahara desert are subjected to temperatures of over one hundred degrees Fahrenheit in the daytime, and below freezing at night. Not surprisingly, the Soninke people of Mauritania tend to spend more time inside their houses than most people spread across the savannah belt of West Africa. This time spent indoors perhaps explains why the Soninke women have excelled in interior decoration. The walls are painted in vibrant colors, most often as long as fifteen to twenty years ago, when the woman first married and was expected to beautify her home. Trade across the Sahara is the Soninke's main contact with the outside world. Because of their commercial isolation, the people tend to be acutely materialistic and collect such items as enamelware, plastic basins, spoons, and rubber sandals. A manifestation of wealth and status, their collections of Western paraphernalia are displayed, accentuating the painted surfaces and complimenting the overall decoration.

Wrought iron beds, complete with mosquito nets and mattresses, have primarily replaced the mud beds or platforms of the past. Aside from their status quality, the western beds do not require maintenance and may be moved around, carried outdoors on cool evenings, or stored depending on the fluctuation of the family size and number of visitors.

The individual Soninke house is U-shaped, the closed side consisting of a long and narrow living room (also used for sleeping) with an entrance facing a large compound shared by all members of the family. On either end of this living space is a corridor, off which are storage rooms and at the end of which is a walled-in courtyard, one side being a pit toilet, the other a private courtyard usually for drying and storing foodstuffs. Several such houses built around the compound and locked together by high mud walls create an organized family settlement with an elaborate entrance gate to keep livestock in and strangers out. The dynamic wall paintings—geometrically composed— are the center point of these domestic spaces. The vibrant colors and quilt-like compositions create a startling contrast to the barren surroundings.

The elaborately painted interior walls of Soninke homes are intensified by the absence of furniture. At most, a bed or a mattress bear witness to a utilized space.
Opposite: A mosquito net hangs over the Medigayi family's bed in a room painted fifteen years ago by a relative, Fenda Gandega. Djajibinni, Mauritania
Above: Habou Camara's living-cum-bedroom. Ouloumbini, Mauritania

Above: Sokhane Camara proudly looks into her home which was painted by in-laws Bonco and Tare Camara. Buanch, Mauritania

Opposite: The main living area of a typical U-shaped dwelling. Corridors at either end of the room lead to separate walled-in, open courtyards at the back of the house. The door on the left leads to subdivided sleeping quarters.

Following pages: Details of two end corridors which lead to open courtyards. The first, with a large water container and row of calabash spoons, was painted by Saloum Camara, the second, by Djeynaba Cisse.

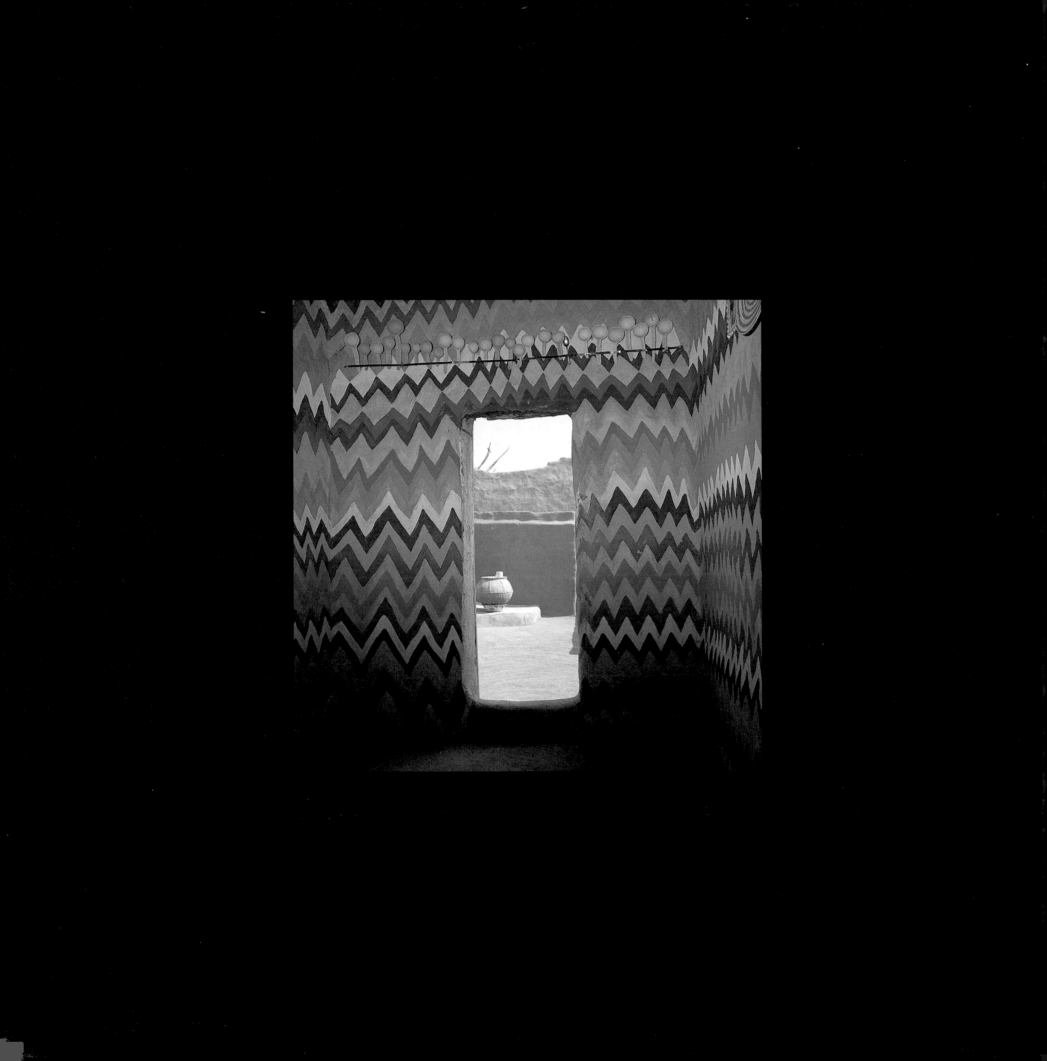

*Opposite and above: Although
artist Khoumba Camara has no
objects to display, she has built
and painted rows of mud
shelving in warm earth tones to
make the room more attractive.
She calls the diamond-shape
motif* contre carreau, *"contrary
to checks." Ouloumbini,
Mauritania.*

Above and opposite: Bonco Camara describes this geometric wall pattern as carreau, *"checks," for a diagonally divided square. Ouloumbini, Mauritania*

*Opposite: A complex, composite
wall painting at the entrance to
Habou Camara's living room,
embracing every motif in the
Soninke's artistic vocabulary.
Ouloumbini, Mauritania*

*Above: Wall detail with
photographs in brightly painted
glass frames, a Senegalese
import*

*Following pages: A detail of the
above wall, incorporating both
the diagonally divided square, or
check—carreau—and the
diamond-shaped contre carreau.*

Above and opposite: After an exhaustive search through thirty-six Soninke villages along the Senegal river, only ruins remain to bear witness to a once prolific and unique painted relief tradition. Ouaoundé, Senegal

Bibliography

Tribal names refer to subgroups or clans and not necessarily their original population group. The Soninke are a subgroup of the Mandingo people who originated in the Niger River area. The Kassena, Nankani, and Kusasi are part of the Gurunsi peoples, also known as Grunne or Fra-Fra, a British derivation of Fara-Fara, a type of greeting. For technical reasons and to simplify reading, orthographic and tonal marks have not been used.
Names of objects and patterns, materials, colors or architectural particulars refer to the local dialect of that particular family or village.

Chesi, Gert. *The Last Africans*. Worgl: Perlinger Verlag, 1977.

Cole, Herbert M. 1968. Mbari is Life. *African Arts 2*, No. 3.

Cole, Herbert M. and Chike C. Aniako. *Igbo Arts: Community and Cosmos*. Los Angeles: Museum of Cultural History, University of California, Los Angeles, 1984.

Cole, Herbert M. and Doran H. Ross. *The Arts of Ghana*. Los Angeles: Museum of Cultural History, University of California, Los Angeles, 1977.

Corral, Jose. *Ciudades de las Caravanas*. Madrid: Editions Hermann Blume, 1985.

Dethier, Jean, ed. *Lehmarchitektur*. Munich: Prestel Verlag, 1982.

Duchemin, G. J. A propos des decorations murales des habitations de Oualata. *Bulletin XII, I.F.A.N.*, 1950.

Du Puigaudeau, O. Contribution á l'etude du symbolisme dans le décor mural et l'artisant de Walâta. *Bulletin XIX, I.F.A.N.*, 1957.

Gardi, Rene. *Maison Africaines: L'Art traditional de batir en Afrique Occidental*. Paris: Elsevier Sequoia, 1974.

Hay, Margaret, and Sharon Stichter, eds. *African Women South of the Sahara*. Harlow: Longman, 1984.

Kepes, Gyorgy, ed. *Education of Vision*. New York: George Braziller, 1965.

Leiris, Michel and Jacqueline Delange. *African Nera*. Milan: Rizzoli, 1967.

Oliver, Paul, ed. *Shelter in Africa*. London: Barrie and Jenkins Ltd., 1971.

Prussin, Labelle. *Architecture in Northern Ghana*. Berkeley: University of California Press, 1969.

———. 1968. The Architecture of Islam in West Africa. *African Arts 1*, No. 2.

———. 1970. Sudanese Architecture and the Manding. *African Arts 3*, No. 4.

Strand, Paul and Basil Davidson. *Ghana: An African Portrait*. New York: Aperture, 1976.

Willis, E. A. *Form and Content in Traditional Uli Painting (MFA Project)*. Nsukka: University of Nigeria, August 1986.

Willet, Frank. *African Art*, London: Thames and Hudson, 1971.

Willet, Frank and Ekpo Eyo. *Treasures of Ancient Nigeria*. New York: Alfred A. Knopf, Inc., 1982.